DARREN LEHMANN

DARREN LEHMANN

Worth the Wait

AN AUTOBIOGRAPHY

Methuen

Published by Methuen 2005

10 9 8 7 6 5 4 3 2 1

First published in Australia in 2004 by
Hardie Grant Books

First published in hardback in the UK by
Methuen Publishing Ltd
215 Vauxhall Bridge Road
London SW1V 1EJ
www.methuen.co.uk

Methuen Publishing Ltd Reg. No. 3543167

ISBN 0 413 77495 3

A CIP catalogue for this title is available from the British Library.

Printed and bound in Great Britain by
St. Edmundsbury Press, Bury St. Edmunds, Suffolk

To my beautiful wife Andrea and my four children, Jake, Tori, Amy and Ethan, who have been so wonderful and supportive while I have pursued my dream.

Also to my Mother, who has sacrificed so much for me. Mum, you have given me so much love and the motivation to strive for my goals. I am truly thankful.

CONTENTS

FOREWORDS

Sometimes in this world of big-business cricket, where sponsorship deals, television ratings and the corporate dollar are valued almost as highly as wickets or runs, it is easy for today's players to lose sight of why we play the game.

The temptation is there to be seduced by the money and fame. The distractions are there to help us forget the reasons we fell in love with cricket as kids, but if ever one needs reminding about what it means to be an international player, they should simply scroll down the Australian batting list and stop at number five. The name will read 'Darren Scott Lehmann' and he will reveal just what it means to pull on the baggy green cap.

From my perspective as Australian captain, 'Boof' sets an example for us all by reinforcing the idea that we play cricket not for riches, but for enjoyment, mateship and the thrill of the contest, the very same values that see kids around the world playing in the park, the backyard or the driveway. That theory was one of many he shared with his great mate David Hookes, who inspired Darren to reach for great heights.

What Darren probably doesn't realise is that he has inspired us all with his courage in dealing with 'Hookesy's' tragic passing and emphasised just how special the camaraderie is among our team. I am proud to call Boof my mate and consider myself honoured to have been asked to contribute to this book.

What he brings to the team is a common-sense, no-nonsense approach, coupled with a fine cricket brain and an eccentric dose of humour. He is always there to provide me with sound advice and in team meetings he is never short of a quick one-liner to liven things up. Every team could do with Darren in its line-up.

While his outlook on life, cricket nous and raw ability to destroy an attack make him a shining example to his team-mates, perhaps the same can't be said about his approach to physical fitness. He somehow manages to avoid the fitness coach and diet experts and his body shape better resembles a beer keg than an elite athlete's.

But that wouldn't worry Boof. Put a beer or smoke in his hand and he is a happy man. Mention the Adelaide Crows and he is even happier. Beer, cigarettes and footy … he is without doubt a throwback to yesterday's cricketer.

But the more I think about Darren's attitude to fitness, the more I realise that it's for a reason. Just prior to last season he thought that, for the first time in his career, he'd try to get himself in shape by running each day. The result? A torn Achilles tendon and an extended stay on the sidelines! I just remember him telling the so-called experts, 'I told you so' and vowing never to subject himself to another fitness regime. Just as well he can bat!

Yet it's that approach that gives him a unique appeal. Saturday afternoon park cricketers probably see a bit of themselves in Boof. He's a player they can relate to.

I'll never forget his First Test hundred, in April 2003 against the West Indies in Trinidad. It epitomised his nature. Once he found his feet, he terrorised a wilting attack in hot Caribbean conditions to reach 160. Fittingly, once he registered triple figures, an Australian fan clambered over the cyclone fence surrounding the ground, raced to the centre and offered him a can of beer. Boof couldn't have scripted the celebration any better.

For a man who has been written off by critics plenty of times, who knows where Darren's cricket will take him given his outstanding run of form. Another World Cup perhaps?

One thing I do know is that whatever he does, it will be done with a smile on his face and without any regrets. That's an example to us all.

Ricky Ponting

How do you write a few serious words about a guy who sports the nicknames 'Boof' and 'Shrek'?

A man who has provided us all with so much entertainment on the cricket field and with so many laughs and great memories as a mate off it.

A bloke who mischief classifies as a close companion, and who is always in the thick of the practical-joke action.

How do you get serious about a bloke who continues to defy all modern science and technology in regards to what it takes to be a 'professional athlete'? Yes, it is a rare occasion when the word 'athlete' is used in a descriptive sense for Darren Lehmann! He's a cricketer who, on scoring brilliant centuries in stifling conditions in the sub-continent, returns to the rooms at lunchbreak, has a couple of cans of soft drink and a few puffs on a cigarette, then goes back out and starts again with minimal fuss.

All this while many of the super-fit 'new-age' players with carefully considered diets and training routines have cramped and crumbled in the very same heat and humidity.

The rare times I've seen Darren Lehmann get even remotely serious have usually been when the beer runs out in the change-rooms or when his beloved Adelaide Crows have suffered a heavy defeat.

But at the start of 2004, Boof, like the rest of the cricketing world, was stunned at the tragic death of his good mate David

Hookes. It was a difficult time as everyone rallied to deal with the shock and sadness, but there are two specific moments I recall that reveal much about Darren and his make-up as a person.

The first was at the Allan Border Medal presentation as rising Aussie singing sensation Shannon Noll was performing an emotional tribute to 'Hooksey'. Although I was sitting next to Darren and his wife Andrea, it was only on the big television screen in the room that I noticed the tears streaming down his face as the pictures were beamed live around the country. Like many in the cricketing world, he was hurting at the death of David and, true to form, he wasn't going to be ashamed to show how he was feeling. Anybody who has dealt with Darren will know there are no hidden agendas; he plays his cards straight and honestly.

The second moment came a month later in Sri Lanka when Darren notched up an outstanding century in the First Test at Galle. Again, there were many people watching via television as he looked to the heavens and acknowledged his absent friend in an emotional tribute. That Darren participated on that tour to Sri Lanka so soon after the Hookes tragedy was quite unbelievable. The courage, desire, and determination he revealed in performing so well are testimony to his strength of character.

Amid all the exquisite drives, deft cut shots and bullish hoicks over backward square, it's that very character that is his greatest strength. It's allowed him to succeed and remain true to himself ... an unchanged view on life and the game, from the time he began until now, fully entrenched in the Test and one-day teams.

Yes, Boof worked out early what works for him and continues to play beautifully the cards he's dealt. So what can I say that is serious about Darren Lehmann?

He is an outstanding guy, a loving husband, a proud father and a loyal friend. He's also one of the funniest, most enjoyable team-mates I've played with.

Seriously.

Adam Gilchrist

Galle, Sri Lanka, March 2004

As the ball went to the fence I felt a massive weight lift off my shoulders. All the crap I had waded through in the past five months was gone and I lifted my eyes and my arms to the heavens and said a silent thanks to my great friend David Hookes, who had died less than three months earlier. I knew he had been looking after me.

When I got into the 90s I had started to think about what a century would mean. I began to think about what it meant to be back in the Aussie team; what it would mean to 'Hookesy', who made his only Test hundred in Sri Lanka; and what it would mean to family and friends who had stuck by me through the tough times. I started to get excited.

When the 100 came, I was totally overcome with emotion. Damien Martyn was my batting partner and I simply grabbed him and couldn't let go. I don't know what I said and I don't remember what he said, but I just clung to him with tears rolling down my face. The relief of the moment was overwhelming and I was very glad 'Marto' was there to hold me up.

I looked up in thanks, and it was as though Hookesy looked down and said in his typical manner, 'You're right now mate, you don't need me any more, off you go, get on with it'.

ONE
EARLY DAYS

There are moments in life when you realise that as long as your bum faces south you are just not going to make it. Until then, you think you are going to get where you want; in fact, when you are young and too naive to know any better, you think it's only a matter of time before you get there. Then one day it can hit you like a bolt of lightning. You realise it's just not going to happen. It comes early for some and there are others who go to their grave convinced they were good enough to achieve something, but they didn't get the breaks.

For me and Australian Rules football this lightning moment came quite early. I was headed for the big time, there was no doubt in my mind – straight into the lofty ranks of league football. From there the sky would be the limit.

I was seventeen and playing for Gawler Centrals (the Tigers) in the Barossa and Light Football League. I was elevated into the reserves for my beloved Central Districts Bulldogs a fortnight later, but this dream run on the road to a long and successful career in league football was brought to a screaming halt after my second senior game. We were absolutely flogged by Port Adelaide and so were the league team.

Aussie Rules legend Neil Kerley was our senior coach and the next night he made us do so many laps of the Elizabeth Oval that I spent more time throwing up over the fence than running. After we finished I dragged myself off the track and fell into the showers. As I was drying myself off, I looked into the mirror and thought, 'Football is just not for me'. And that was it: I retired from the game that night and haven't played since.

A brilliant career nipped in the bud? I don't think so. Don't get me wrong, I wanted to play, but all those bloody 100-metre sprints ... and if we lost they flogged us. It was bloody hard work and I just didn't have the passion.

In hindsight it was a smart decision. I loved footy and I still do. I am a massive fan of the Adelaide Crows and given the choice would actually far rather watch them than any game of cricket. But I was never going to be as good at football as cricket and, I had to be honest, the workload was never going to agree with me.

Like any kid growing up in country Australia in the 1970s, there were two things more important to me than anything else (except family, of course): football and cricket. Because I was born and raised in South Australia, Australian Rules football was the only code in winter and there was cricket in summer. I played my first game of cricket at age seven for Whyalla South. Whyalla is a country town two hours north of Adelaide and my father Trevor was the local policeman. By the time I was ten I was playing for the Whyalla South Under 14s, a side that was captained by Peter Gladigau, the fast bowler who went on to play for South Australia.

But they were just the organised games; I would actually play cricket all day, every day, either against the other kids in the neighbourhood or in the backyard by myself. I would throw a golf ball against the back wall and hit it with a cricket bat. I wasn't good enough to go with a stump like Sir Donald Bradman, but I had a cut-down bat and flower pots positioned around the back garden that served as fieldsmen. I would bat right-handed and left-handed – Ian Chappell one minute, Rod Marsh the next. I was always playing for Australia and, don't worry, we always won. I loved pretending to wear the baggy green and hooking everyone from Ian Botham to Bob Willis.

Then when I got to school, the whole lunchbreak in summer would be taken up playing cricket, either on the school oval or a practice session that would consist of the batsman batting until someone could get him out. The same would happen with Aussie Rules in winter.

As you can probably gather, there wasn't a lot of homework done; in fact, I would go as far as to say there was none. School was just an annoying interruption between recess, lunch and the end of school – when we played sport.

Children today have a lot more to do. I see this with my own kids. They have computers, electronic games and television. And there are so many sports available. Basketball, soccer, lacrosse, softball and t-ball were almost unheard of where I grew up. There may have been a tennis court or two some-where, but no-one ever used them, and golf was an old man's game. The boys in my town all played footy and cricket, and the girls played netball.

Another thing that has changed dramatically since I was young is the concern about children's safety. Back then we would roam the streets of Whyalla looking for local kids to make up a team and when we found them we would head to the oval and play for hours. Unfortunately now, wandering the streets looking for mates to play cricket is a thing of the past.

I was lucky to be brought up in a country town where everyone knew everyone and the sporting culture was enormous. It was the perfect environment for my early days. My father moved jobs and we came back to town when I was eleven. Well, nearer to town anyway; we built a house in Gawler, forty minutes north of Adelaide. It was the start of some great times.

I made some great friends who I still catch up with from time to time, guys like Andrew Warland, Darren Joyce and Tony Skuse, as well as schoolmates like Johnny Giannetto and John Abbott. We played cricket and footy, and did all the things teenagers do. Between us we made as much fun as possible.

I started playing junior cricket for any side I could get my hands on – Gawler, Sandy Creek and Lyndoch. I wouldn't say I was the best player in every team I played in, but I was generally in the top two or three and it was after playing well in those teams that I was selected to play in the local representative under-age team.

A couple more good performances later, I wound up in the South Australian Under-13 team. I was frustrated that I had never made a hundred, but I finally achieved it when I was thirteen and promptly kissed the pitch at Gawler South.

This was no meteoric rise by the way; any good young cricketer in South Australia at the time was playing in the local representative primary school competition called SAPSARSA. There would be few first-class cricketers in the modern era from South Australia who didn't make their way through that competition when they were in their early teens. If you played well in the SAPSARSA competition you were chosen in the

State team for your age. It was that selection that got me to Salisbury Cricket Club, a place I would almost call home for the next decade.

Salisbury was pretty much the powerhouse of the Adelaide district competition for much of the time I was there. They had top-rank players like Peter Sleep, Glenn Bishop, Bob Zadow, Harvey Jolly and Wayne Bradbrook, as well as Wayne Prior, the fastest bowler in the State and a player who had appeared in World Series Cricket. He was in the first team when I arrived at the club, so you can imagine it was a pretty intimidating place to be at age fourteen.

Out in the working-class suburban belt, the Salisbury club was far from wealthy and definitely didn't carry any pretensions about where it fitted in the overall scheme of things. But from my point of view the best thing about playing there was that I was pushed through from an early age. I was marched up the grades quicker than I would have been at another club.

I have never played a D- or C-grade game in my life; from the moment I got there I was playing juniors in the morning and second team cricket in the afternoon. At the age of fourteen I made two hundreds in the second team and the following year I was elevated to the A-grade side. Here I was, fifteen, and playing with the blokes I just mentioned and against players like David Hookes and Wayne Phillips. I was in awe, even a little scared, but very excited by it all.

Looking back, it was extraordinary for a kid that young to be playing cricket at that level. But it was also the best thing that could have happened to me. Playing from a young age with and against adults made me a much better player and person. I have no doubt about that. In my opinion it was and still is the best way to learn any game, by playing against people older and better than you.

Look at tennis players like Lleyton Hewitt and Pat Rafter – from a young age they competed against players much older and better ranked. With that as their schooling, it didn't take them long to work their way up the ladder. Golfer Aaron Baddeley winning the Australian Open while still in his teens and Ricky Ponting exploding onto the scene as a sixteen-year-old are further examples.

Some people argue that it's better to hold young talent back. Maybe that's right in a game like football or rugby where the opposition are much bigger and stronger and you can be seriously hurt if you are too young, but in games like cricket, as soon as young players show they are ready, send them up there, I say. They will learn more from playing with men than they ever will dominating against kids their own age.

That was the great thing about being at Salisbury; the club challenged me to take the next step. Most fifteen-year-olds back then were playing at school and here I was up against some of the best cricketers in the country. There were big, strong and at times intimidating men and in that company you grow up fast. You have no choice and it's not just on the field where you do your learning. In the dressing room after play, I would have beers (not many or the old man would have killed me) with men more than twice my age, men who had represented their State and country. That's where you learn about cricket and life, from the mouths of these men who have well and truly been there and done that.

But it was strange at times. I remember that my physical education teacher in Year 10 at school was a guy called Peter

Cameron, who was also my team-mate at Salisbury. Here I was playing with him on weekends, swearing, at times drinking and generally having a whale of a time. But at 9 a.m. on Monday mornings he was my teacher. To make matters worse, he failed me, but I deserved it. I spent more time playing football and cricket. But he was terrific, as was the whole club. The people accepted me straightaway and made it very easy for a kid with pimples to feel like he was part of the team.

I am sure that the generosity of the management and players at Salisbury Cricket Club was the sole reason I started playing at the first-class level so early. I was in the right place at the right time, but those men at Salisbury can take a lot of the credit; they believed in me before I believed in myself.

By this I mean I was in the situation I wanted. I was playing grade cricket and I wanted to play for my State, but had no idea that it would happen so quickly. Inevitably, with a cricket career charging ahead, something had to give and for me that something was school.

School and I were never a good match – I didn't want to be there and I wasn't listening when I should have been. When you are counting down the minutes to the bell you aren't learning much. Come my sixteenth birthday I was out of there.

I regret this enormously now. If I had my time again I know I would have worked a lot harder. I will certainly be pushing my children to dedicate themselves to their studies a lot more than I did. I am not saying high educational qualifications are everything, but if you have none it really limits what you can do. I was lucky that the cricket thing worked, because I really didn't have much to fall back on and that was a mistake.

But as one door closes another opens, just as they say. It so happened that the father of one of my mates at the cricket club was a manager of one of the departments at the Holden car manufacturing plant in Elizabeth. I fronted up for an interview and was lucky enough to get a job on the assembly line making the legendary Holden cars. Now some people may think that lucky isn't the right word, but I absolutely loved my time working for Holden. The people out there were sensational, salt of the earth and, as at the cricket club, they really took me under their wing. There were blokes out there who had been assembling struts and axles for fifty years and there I was, a sixteen-year-old kid, sidling up next to them.

I used to get $250 before tax a week and that was a king's ransom for a guy in his teens. I was still living at home and work used to start at seven in the morning and finish at three in the afternoon, which was perfect because I had more than enough time to get to training. The managers at Holden were also great, allowing me to take leave without pay when I went away to play cricket for South Australia in the under-age teams. It was the perfect set-up for me and I worked there very happily for the next eighteen months. I thought I was the luckiest kid alive.

My fondest memories of the Holden plant were the days when it was really hot. It was forty degrees outside and that translated into about sixty in the shed. When it got that bad I used to slip an automatic gearbox into a manual car, sort of 'accidentally on purpose', and that would shut down the line down for half an hour. The bosses used to crack it but the boys loved me because we would all go outside and stand under the tree, which was a damned site cooler than the production line.

Life at that stage was pretty rosy. I was earning money, I was playing a great standard of cricket and I was surrounded by people who loved and cared for me both at home and at work. I look back on those times as some of the happiest in my life. It was for this reason that I turned down a position in the first intake of the Australian Institute of Sport's Cricket Academy.

It was the first time in my life that I had to sit down and take stock of where I was headed. Before being invited to the Academy I had just drifted along happily, allowing one thing to lead to another because I generally ended up in a good place. But here came an offer to completely uproot my life and join fifteen other young players in a dormitory-style place, living and breathing cricket every day.

It may sound like something that a young bloke should jump at but you need to remember that I was playing first-class cricket, content at work and still living at home. To take the offer and join the Academy I needed to throw all that in and completely change a life I absolutely loved. I was reluctant to do that. At that stage the Academy hadn't started and no-one knew what it was going to be like. In later years, under the guidance of the great Rod Marsh, it was a wonderful place to spend a year but back in the mid-1980s it was a complete unknown.

My thinking was that I was already learning from the likes of David Hookes and Andrew Hilditch – and you can throw Peter Sleep and Wayne Phillips in there as well. Surely they could teach me anything I didn't know?

I sought some guidance from people whose opinion I trusted, including Hookes, Ian Chappell and even Richie Benaud. They all said to not go. They said I had a balanced life, I was already playing very good cricket and I was among family and friends. 'Why would you change that for anything?' they asked and I must say I wholeheartedly agreed with them.

People ask me now whether I regret not going to the Academy and I say 'No, not then'. I would love to be seventeen again and able to go when Rod Marsh was in charge because I saw the job he did and the way the young players were guided. It would have been superb. But when it was my turn it wasn't the right time, simple as that, and given my time again I would have done exactly the same thing.

I wasn't the only player to turn down a spot in that first year. James Brayshaw, later my South Australian team-mate, also knocked it back because he was a cadet journalist in Perth and wanted to pursue that career.

The funny thing about the Academy and that initial offer was my mum had sent the application form in without me knowing. She was desperate for me to become part of it and was devastated when I turned it down. She probably still thinks to this day I didn't play for Australia earlier because I didn't go to the Academy. You know what, maybe she is right.

Did it hurt me later on? Maybe. Did players from the Academy get picked before me because they had gone? Maybe. How would you ever know? I would like to think that wasn't the case.

In life you do the things that feel right at the time. People call it gut instinct (and gut is something I have plenty of) and at the time mine was to let it pass. Anyway, my motto in life is never look back. Once you make a decision it's made and you go on and try to make it work.

So I stayed playing for Salisbury and really didn't give the Academy too much more thought. I did leave Holden not too long after that to work in a local sports store called Roberts &

Jarman. That's something I regret, not because the people at the sports store were bad – in fact, they were fantastic – but because I left Holden for the wrong reasons.

I thought it would look better if I worked for a sports store. I got an offer from Roberts & Jarman and for some reason I'd always wanted to work in a sports store, among all that shiny new sports gear. I had fun there, but I had loved it at Holden and the people there were so good to me. I honestly don't think I realised how important a part of my young life they had been until I left.

I see young cricketers now playing for South Australia and Yorkshire who have little else in their lives. At eighteen and nineteen they only play cricket. That puts a lot of pressure on young people to succeed at a sport that is already difficult enough.

For me, good day or bad day on the field, I still had to front up to work at seven in the morning on Monday. Don't worry, if I'd had a bad day the boys at Holden all knew about it. They would cut my score out if I made a duck and plaster it right in front of where they knew I would be working. They would offer all sorts of advice. Fat sixty-year-old blokes who had never been on a cricket field in their life would wander up and suggest I give the hook shot away or eat more steak on the morning of the game. It was a great leveller because you couldn't get carried away with yourself in front of these blokes. They would bring you down to earth quick smart.

The same men, though, would be so proud of you when you succeeded. I vividly remember the day I was selected to play for South Australia for the first time and the Channel Nine camera crew came out to the factory floor. The workers were over the moon and they made me feel ten foot tall.

That's what working does for you when you are a young sportsman. It keeps you grounded and it keeps a perspective in your life at a time when you really need it. Sport is important in life, but working alongside men in their fifties who have to work every day putting axles together to feed their wife and three kids and pay the mortgage will definitely keep your feet glued to the ground.

If I could change one thing about sport today it would be to find a way for young cricketers and footballers and any other team sport players to stay in the workforce while they are making their way through the grades. Cricket is nowhere near as much fun when your ability to pay the bills depends on it and life is a pretty shallow place when you spend all your time mixing with people who play the same sport professionally.

I think back to those days from time to time now that I have moved on and I realise how lucky I was to have been exposed to those people at that stage of my life. Those men at Holden taught me there was a whole other world out there and it was a world full of really cool people who had absolutely nothing to do with cricket. They didn't play it, didn't watch it and couldn't have given a stuff about it, yet they were ripping men and women. They liked me for who I was.

I just wonder if the young people playing professional sport today are missing out by not experiencing something similar when they leave school. That said, I am sure if I was seventeen today I would be doing exactly what they are doing. What kid wouldn't jump at the chance of playing full time the sport they love and getting paid for it?

I didn't know it at the time, but that life wasn't far away for me in 1987. At seventeen I was about to step through into a world that would become my playground for the next seventeen years. When I look back on it now I cannot believe I got the phone call and I still cannot properly get my head around the roller-coaster ride that followed.

TWO
STATE
CAP
FITS

The first inkling I had that something big was about to happen was in my second year of A-grade cricket in 1987. I had just made a double century against East Torrens and a century preceding that in another district game – out of nowhere people were suddenly starting to talk about 'this kid Darren Lehmann'.

I had been playing in the first team at Salisbury, making the occasional 50, batting in the middle order and starting to really enjoy playing cricket at that level. Then these big scores started to appear. People sit up and take notice any time a player makes a century and follows it up with a double century in the grade competition, so you can imagine what it was like when that someone was a seventeen-year-old. I went from complete obscurity to the talk of the town and with that came attention from the people who matter most in a young cricketer's life: the selectors.

So down we went to Glenelg Oval, or the 'bay' as it was known, for the next match and there to watch was Murray Sargent, a man who had been chairman of selectors for longer than I had been alive. The pressure was on and it turned out I played pretty well and made 80. Glenelg had Mike Haysman, a State player, in its side and that probably helped. To make runs in front of State players never did you any harm and I was happy to get some while both he and a State selector were watching.

Anyway, after the game Murray Sargent came up to me and I was thinking he might be going to say something like 'Well played' or 'Keep it going', the sort of encouraging stuff selectors generally say to young players. But all he said was: 'Young man, those boots are a disgrace. You should make sure they are clean before walking out on the ground!'

I was shattered. It was a pretty ordinary thing to say to a young bloke, in my opinion. I had played well and I wasn't expecting a fashion tip. Given that dressing down, I didn't think I was next in line for the Sheffield Shield team.

But you know what? I have never forgotten what he said and to this day I have never paid undue attention to my appearance. I suppose it's the rebellious streak in me. Back then I just thought, 'Stuff you mate, I'll wear what I feel comfortable in'. And as for the boots, well, Mum took control of them after that. She would be there every Saturday morning with the whitener, making sure they were spick and span each time I took the field. I would tell her they looked fine, but mums are mums, I guess, and I think Murray's comment hurt her far more than it did me.

These days I think selecting is a pretty thankless task. Very few players ever thank you for selecting them but plenty abuse you when they get dropped. The other thing people regularly overlook when discussing the merits of selectors is that they receive absolutely no pay. They travel each week, giving up their own time to watch players and assess new talent. But at that particular stage I was in awe of selectors; they were well and truly people to whom you spoke only when spoken to.

So when I received the call from Murray Sargent asking if I could come down to State training, I was in complete shock – I had been selected in the side to play against Victoria in Melbourne!

I remember turning to Mum in the kitchen and telling her I'd been chosen in the State side.

She said, 'Oh that's good, love, what's that – the Under 19s?'

I said, 'No, the State side.'

All the colour drained out of her face. She just looked at me blankly and after a moment said, 'What, to play with David Hookes?'

'Yes,' I replied.

We just stood there in the kitchen, staring at each other. I don't think either of us could believe it. Then we jumped around the room like two kids on Christmas Day. She was so proud. My father was much more laidback. His line of thinking was always 'If he's good enough he'll get there', whereas Mum wore her heart on her sleeve. She was always very nervous when I was playing and extremely biased when it came to her son and his cricket.

I remember her sitting me down before we left on the plane and demanding that I say 'Please' and 'Thank you', use the correct knife and fork, be in bed by a certain time and show the people around me respect. I felt like I was going off to boarding school, but looking back she was just desperate that I make the most of an amazing opportunity. She is quite incredible, my Mother, and I love her very much. She gave up her social life for me to pursue cricket and I will always be indebted to her.

When I went for training at the Adelaide Oval, I was hugely excited but also very nervous. At that stage I didn't think I was going to be playing in the game; I assumed I would be the twelfth man, which was the normal way for young players to be introduced to the State team. But when I got there that changed very quickly. Trevor Robertson was the coach of South Australia at the time and a couple of the little things he said made me think, 'Hang on, there's more to this'.

Then the captain, David Hookes, walked straight up to me and said, 'Congratulations kid, you're in the side and will be batting number six!'

I nearly fell over. I can hardly even remember what I said to him. It was almost unreal. I think I must have said something about looking forward to it and thanks for the chance. There was I thinking I was just going to be making up the numbers and suddenly I was being fitted out with armfuls of South Australian equipment and I was going to play! I was given the sensational red cap, a helmet, two jumpers, training gear and a travel uniform. I'm sure my feet didn't touch the ground for the rest of the night.

Another great thing about playing in this game was that my team-mate from Salisbury, Harvey Jolly, also made his debut. We had played all of our grade cricket together and it made the whole thing extra special to have my mate along for the ride. Our positions in the South Australian side had become available because Tim May and Peter Sleep had been elevated to the Australian side for the Test match against New Zealand.

There were even a couple more familiar faces to make things easier. Amazingly, another seventeen-year-old was playing. Shane George had burst onto the scene earlier in the year and was impressing everyone with his pace. We had played a lot of junior cricket, with and against each other, a few years earlier.

My old mate from the Whyalla South days, Peter Gladigau, was also in the side. That had been some journey for the two of us, playing together in a small country town and now for our State at the famous MCG. Instead of feeling totally intimidated in a first-class team full of grown men, not to mention a few legends, having Peter and Shane around made it a little less terrifying.

Back then, as a youngster in a Sheffield Shield team, you were definitely to be seen but not heard. And I was way too scared to ever say anything to the captain, Hookes. He was a superstar in my eyes, a man who had taken on Tony Greig in the Centenary Test in 1977 and famously smashed him for five fours in a row. He had been the pin-up boy of World Series Cricket and he basically controlled South Australian cricket at that time.

I had often travelled down from Gawler on the train to the Adelaide Oval just to watch Hookes bat, and from the other side of the fence I used to think, 'One day I am going to bat like that'. He just had a way about him that appealed to me. I think I even stole his signature loft over mid-wicket, a shot he played that showed the bowler nothing but contempt.

However terrified I was of David, he was always great to me. He was there whenever I needed advice, he always encouraged me to be the best I could be, and above all he was a very good friend. But back then he was 'the man' and I didn't feel fit to clean his boots.

So off I went, a kid from Gawler, on my first interstate tour, to play my first Sheffield Shield game against the old enemy Victoria at the most famous cricket ground in the world, the 'G'. People in England may argue that Lord's is the most famous, but I disagree. The MCG was the place where the First Test match was played, in 1877. It also hosted the 1956 Olympic Games and of course continues to host all the Boxing Day Test matches and Australian Rules football grand finals.

My earliest memory of the tour was my room-mate, Andrew Hilditch, the South Australian vice-captain who had also been vice-captain of Australia just a few years earlier. 'Digger' and I were like chalk and cheese; he was well-spoken, well-educated and, away from cricket, a member of the legal profession. His wife was the daughter of then-Australian coach Bob Simpson and he was an established first-class cricketer.

I was none of those things, but Hilditch took me under his wing. He made sure I was on time for everything and told me what to do and, more importantly, what not to do in the dressing room, like not speaking out of turn or making silly comments. When it came to going into the opposition rooms for a beer he took me in and introduced me to the members of the Victorian team. This was a time-honoured tradition, allowing youngsters the opportunity to listen and learn from the greats of the game. Sadly, this happens less often today due to the demands of professional sport.

Looking back, whoever made the decision to put me in the same room as Andrew Hilditch must have known something, because he couldn't have been more helpful or made me feel more at home in the team. His example is one I have since tried to follow with young players coming into sides I play in. Of course, things are a bit different now; players often get their own rooms or apartments rather than share.

I remember arriving at the hotel room in Melbourne and opening my bag, which had been packed by Mum, to find all my clothes pristinely ironed – it must have taken her hours! I started to lay my gear out but Digger said it was time to introduce ourselves to the man behind the bar. This was a Sheffield Shield tradition: you would arrive wherever you were playing, dump your gear and head straight to the bar for a drink. It's amazing how times have changed; if you tried that today you'd be sent home.

But down I went to the bar, to join the men I would be playing with, heroes like David Hookes, Wayne Phillips and Mike Haysman, who were offering to buy me a drink. I didn't say a word; I just listened to them telling stories and talking about the approaching match. I had idolised David and Wayne (being left-handers) since I was a boy.

During the game we sat in the viewing area watching, but I was too in awe to concentrate on what was happening in the middle. All I could think about was how much fun it all was and how cool these guys were.

I wore a helmet for the first time in my life that day and I only wore it because almost everyone else did. Hookes gave me heaps about it (he didn't wear one): he said I should play the same way I played at home, with a cap on, but I just felt it was right to wear one. It would save my life in Perth a couple of games later, so I made the right decision. But I remember thinking how stupid I looked as I put it on, especially with my mullet haircut, which was the fashion then. But I got used to the 'lid' soon enough.

So there I was, next in to bat, watching Hookes and Phillips belting a pretty good Victorian attack that included Tony Dodemaide and Simon Davis, both of whom had played for Australia. Suddenly 'Hookesy' got out and I was in. My heart started racing; in fact, I don't even remember getting from the dressing rooms to the centre.

Then, as still happens today while I wait to bat – no matter how big the occasion or how nervous I feel – as soon as I got to the centre I felt good. Dodemaide was bowling and he was waiting at the top of his mark while I asked for middle and leg. Phillips was at the other end and offered words of encouragement. I thought, 'Well, this is it!' The pitch was pretty flat and the bowlers were tired after Hookes and Phillips had finished with them, so it was a good time to go out and bat. I batted for about half an hour, facing Dodemaide and the left-arm finger spin of Paul Jackson.

I got off the mark with a 4, leg-glanced to the Bay 13 boundary (this was in the days before the Great Southern Stand) off Dodemaide, and I cover drove another boundary before being out, caught in close off Jackson.

And that was it. My Sheffield Shield debut brought me the massive sum of 10 runs. In horseracing terms, I think you could say I would be better for the run. The whole experience was overwhelming and in hindsight I don't think I was mature enough to put the hype aside and just do what I do best: focus on the ball and hit it. I still can't believe I got out bat-pad to a spinner. In fact, I reckon in nearly twenty years of first-class cricket I've only been out that way a handful of times.

But that was that, I was out. Sitting in the rooms, taking my gear off, I was thinking, 'Wait till I get back out there, I am going to show those bastards – they haven't seen the best of me!' What I didn't know then was that it would take me more than six months to make it back out to the centre of any first-class arena, let alone the MCG, as after that game Peter Sleep and Tim May returned and I wasn't picked again for the rest of the season.

I was devastated, although of course I realised I was never going to get a game before May and Sleep. I could just hear the hierarchy saying: 'He's done his job. We've given him a game – now let's pack him off back to grade cricket so we don't have to worry about him for the rest of the year'.

I think at that age you take things like that very personally, you read much more into them than is actually there. I realise now that being dropped was the best thing that could have happened because it lit a fire in my belly. I had been given a taste of the good stuff and I wanted more. For the first time in my cricketing life I had something to prove. I wasn't just playing for fun; I was playing to show people I was good enough.

That culminated in the grand final of the district competition that year when Salisbury chased the 400-plus set by David Hookes' East Torrens team. I got 80 not out to get us home. It may have been a district game, but it won us the final and it was a special feeling to make those runs in front of David, in a big game, and to play a part in winning us the flag.

I felt confident that 1988–89 was going to be a good season and it certainly got off on the right foot. Barry Richards was appointed coach for South Australia and turned out to be a great influence on me. Right from the beginning he included me in everything: the State squad, full training – the lot. I really had the sense that he wanted me to succeed and it's amazing what a motivating effect that has on you when you are young, especially coming from such a legend.

Barry played just four Tests against Australia in 1969–70 before South Africa was banned from the game due to apartheid. He had an average in the 70s and then never played at that level again – a tragedy for cricket. He once made 356 at the WACA ground against a West Australian bowling attack that comprised Dennis Lillee, Graham McKenzie and Tony Lock. And he made 325 of those in one day! Apparently on the last ball of the day he walked down the wicket to the great Lillee, who was bowling with the new ball, smacked it straight back over his head, one bounce into the fence, and kept walking to the dressing rooms without breaking stride.

To have someone like that encouraging you was a huge boost. He had a great way with people, especially those who were perhaps not your normal style of player. I had never been properly coached as a kid. I didn't move my feet a lot; I just stood there and hit the ball when it arrived. I probably didn't play straight enough in the early days and I probably played too many shots too early, but Barry never tried to change any of that.

Neither did my other mentors from that time, David Hookes and my skipper at Salisbury, Wayne Bradbrook. In fact, all my coaches, from my first to the latest (Wayne Phillips), have always been incredibly supportive of my natural style. Their advice was always along the lines of 'if you are good enough, go for it'. It suited me just fine.

When the season got underway I felt in really good shape to

make the next step and start sorting this Sheffield Shield cricket out. I didn't know it was going to take another three months and five Shield games before I would get a second chance.

At the start of the summer I was in the squad but not in the team. Paul Nobes had enjoyed a big summer the year before, winning the Bradman Medal for the best player in the district competition, and he was selected in front of me. I had no problem with that but I did have a problem with the fact that South Australia had no wins on the board from our first five games. Only Nobes was making any runs and I *still* wasn't getting a game. I had made five centuries for Salisbury in the district and local one-day competitions. I thought I was well and truly ready to be selected but they kept leaving me out.

For South Australia the season was basically over, as we had no chance of reaching the finals in either the Shield or one-day competition. In that sense it was a good time to come in because opportunities were there for the young players without the pressure of finals. Barry Richards and Hookesy were both pushing for me. It was the right time to be picked and start trying to cement a place.

The first game I was picked to play in very nearly became my last.

We went to Perth to play against the awesome West Australian side that had won the Shield the previous summer and would go on to win three in a row. They had Graeme Wood, Geoff Marsh, Kim Hughes, Terry Alderman, Bruce Reid, Chris Matthews, Tom Moody, Tom Hogan, Ken Macleay and Mike Veletta all in the side. In other words, ten of their starting eleven had played for Australia and five of them were in the international team at the time. No wonder they were winning everything on offer.

So that was the scene for my second game, a fast WACA pitch against arguably the best domestic bowling attack in the world.

We lost the toss, were sent in to bat and found ourselves three for 0 with Hilditch, Hookes and Glenn Bishop, our most experienced players, back in the pavilion.

Out I went to face Bruce Reid and Terry Alderman. It was seriously a case of sending a boy to do a man's job. Alderman was darting the ball all over the place into the wind and Reid was bowling fast at the other end. Very few people realise that in his early days before injury pulled him up, Reid was at times a genuinely fast bowler. This was one of those times.

I hadn't been out there long when I was hit in the head by a ball I still to this day am convinced I never saw. It was fast, delivered from about eight foot and it crashed into my helmet, right where it was protecting my right temple.

I am very glad I didn't listen to Hookesy's advice from the year before about wearing a helmet because I am sure that if I hadn't had it on, I would have been seriously injured or per-haps even killed. As it was, I was knocked out cold.

I fell back into the arms of the short-leg fieldsman, James Brayshaw, who told me afterwards that my eyes had rolled back. He was trying to get my helmet off and telling me to breathe – he thought I was dead. I was laid flat out just off the WACA pitch and players came running from everywhere.

I have been told all this, I don't remember any of it and that's probably a good thing. I think if I had remembered I probably would have taken a long time to recover mentally.

As you can imagine, I wasn't feeling too confident going into the next game in Adelaide. I'd played two games, been knocked over for ten in Melbourne and knocked out for not too many more in Perth. On the flight home from Perth I vividly recall sitting on the plane and thinking, 'I'm not good enough to play at this level, I'm just not up to it'. I was eighteen, I had played two matches and they were memorable for all the wrong reasons.

Thankfully I couldn't dwell on those thoughts for long because we had a game against New South Wales starting as soon as we arrived home. To my absolute delight I managed to get rolling in that match; I finally started batting like the Darren Lehmann I recognised and I felt great.

New South Wales had a very good attack, spearheaded by Mike Whitney and Geoff Lawson. Greg Matthews was in there as well.

But I was back at home and I was in the groove for the first time in that company. The drives were finding the gaps and the cut shots that I played with my eyes closed at grade level were finding the fence. I had that feeling that I was invincible, that it didn't matter what they bowled, it was going to the fence. That, funnily enough, was pretty much what happened. I hit the first ball I faced from Geoff Lawson for four and I was away.

I screamed to 40, most of my runs coming from boundaries, and I felt sensational when I brought up my first half-century for South Australia. The hair stood up on the back of my neck when I heard the applause.

But elation very quickly turned to fury.

Lawson was bowling around the wicket to Hilditch and we

set off for a comfortable single after Digger stroked the ball into the covers. With Lawson bowling around the wicket to a right-hander, to chase the ball he had to cut across the line where I was running. He did exactly that and in my opinion slowed down just enough to clip me on the way past, basically tripping me, so that I fell flat on my face. There were gloves and bats flying everywhere. It actually looked very funny on the replay, but there was no humour to be had at the time.

I was on the ground as the throw went to Greg Dyer, the New South Wales captain and wicketkeeper, who took off the bails. I was miles out of my ground. The Blues appealed and I was given out, though I had no doubt I had been deliberately tripped. Technically this was the correct decision, because in the strict interpretation of the rules it was out. But Dyer turned to Lawson and told him he didn't want the appeal to stand because he, like I and the 6000 other people at the ground, thought it wasn't in the spirit of the game.

Lawson told his captain either the appeal stood or he wasn't going to bowl. So that was me cooked – I was sent packing, run out for 50.

I can still remember the booing from the crowd as I walked off the ground. They were furious and so was I. But if you added up the fury of everyone and put mine on top, it still wouldn't have matched that of our skipper, Hookes. To say he had steam coming out of his ears was an understatement. He was breathing fire.

He and Geoff Lawson had never really got on well at the best of times on the field. I have no idea how they got on after hours, but when they locked horns on the field it was never friendly. Declarations gone wrong and differing interpretations of the grey areas of the game's rules had littered their past and this was destined to be another chapter.

I got into the dressing rooms, sat down and started to take my gear off before being confronted by Hookesy and Barry Richards.

'Why the hell did you walk off?' they wanted to know.

'Because the umpire gave me out,' I replied.

'But that wasn't out,' Hookesy raged. 'You were cheated out, he deliberately tripped you over!'

Soon came the tea-break and as the New South Wales players walked up the race, Hookesy was waiting for them – especially for Lawson. A massive argument ensued – Hookesy giving it to Lawson and Dyer, saying they were a disgrace and ought to be ashamed of themselves. Lawson fired back, Mike Whitney stepped in to defend his fast-bowling mate and it started to get pretty ugly, and the top of the race at the Adelaide Oval isn't a big area.

In the end cooler heads prevailed and the match went on, but it was something I didn't forget quickly.

Three games into my Sheffield Shield career and I felt I had been through the wringer, well and truly. However, the key thing to come out of that home game against New South Wales was I had started to play well.

In the final three games of that season I made an 80 in the return match against the Blues in Sydney, another 80 against Victoria at the MCG (with Merv Hughes steaming in) and a 70 in Hobart against Tasmania.

I really felt after the last game that I had taken a massive step towards cementing my place in the South Australian line-up. But, more importantly, I thought I had started to bat 'my way' against the best bowlers in the land. My game, the one that had been so successful at the lower levels, was going to work at the first-class level. I was sure of it and that was the thought I took into the summer of 1989.

THREE
GOLDEN
SUMMER

There are times in your life as a sportsman where you just click, times when everything just falls into place and you have absolutely no idea why. The reason I can confidently say you have no idea why is this: if you knew, you would make it that way all the time. No, I am sure that the 'zone', as it's sometimes called, comes and goes and the best thing you can do when it's there is ride it as hard and long as you can. It won't last forever; only one batsman in the history of the game managed to make it last for a whole career and Sir Donald Bradman was a freak case, simple as that.

Everyone else, and I am talking about greats here, such as Viv Richards and Greg Chappell, goes through patches where they just can't get out and then, for no apparent reason, through patches where they find making runs dreadfully difficult.

It's one of the things, in my opinion, that makes cricket such an amazing game. You can be the best player in the world and you can be knocked over by a part-time medium pacer in a social game. It's unlikely, but it does happen.

That doesn't occur in almost any other sport. Lleyton Hewitt would never lose to the pennant champion at the local tennis club, Ian Thorpe could swim feet first and still beat the district swimming-club champ and the 'Oarsome Foursome' at their best would beat any rowing four put up against them.

But cricket is different. Umpires hold a batsman's fate in their hands and then there is luck, and people who think luck doesn't play a huge part in batting are kidding themselves. How many times have you seen a player batting and he plays and misses every second ball he faces? Then a new batsman comes in and edges the first good ball he receives to the keeper and he's on his way.

It's a fickle game and it can turn on you very quickly.

But there are times when the cricket gods smile on you and mine came in the summer of 1989–90. Right from the get-go I was seeing the ball like a watermelon. I made 228 against New South Wales in the first Sheffield Shield game of the season and followed that up with a century in the second match. I then made 90 against the touring team and after that came a century in the third Shield game and another in the fourth. Basically, by Christmas I had made close to 700 first-class runs, averaging 100 per innings and included in that tally were four first-class centuries and a double century. The only time I had 'missed out' in a match was when I made a 90 against the touring New Zealanders and I will take that as a miss any day of the week.

It was a golden run; I couldn't put a foot wrong. Every shot seemed to find the gap and every time the ball went in the air it missed a fielder and went for four. I was playing shots I didn't think I was capable of and they were all coming off.

The other incredible thing about this purple patch was the rate I was scoring at. Hundreds were coming up in two hours almost every time. If I faced a hundred balls I was either close to a century or had passed it.

It was also then that I started to get to know a person who would become one of my best and most loyal friends.

Barry 'Nugget' Rees is a legend in South Australia. In fact, some would say he is legendary throughout Australia, and I think they are right. He has been a part of the furniture in the South Australian and Australian dressing rooms since the 1960s. His story starts some forty years ago when Australian wicketkeeper Barry Jarman took him under his wing and gave him a job at his sports store Rowe & Jarman. Nugget started as a storeman and has since become one of the most loved and recognised figures in the city of Adelaide. He can't walk down the street without people stopping him to say hello.

Every day's play at the Adelaide Oval sees Nugget in the home side's dressing rooms providing drinks, chewing gum and encouragement – whatever it takes. Never has anyone in the history of South Australian cricket been a more devoted fan and the players absolutely love him. The South Australian team takes him on an away trip once a year. Players in the State side have been doing this for many years. He always gets to have a bat at the end of a game, and he always seems to get a 100 runs everywhere he plays.

He is unashamedly one-eyed. If you are batting and you get out for a duck, even if all three stumps are lying on the ground, Nugget will tell you it was a bad decision. He will say it must have been a no-ball. Players throughout the decades have loved Nugget so much that when he was honoured with a roast at the Adelaide Oval, more than 500 people turned up to pay tribute. The assembled guest speakers read like a who's who of Australian cricket, with people like Ian and Greg

Chappell, Steve Waugh, Merv Hughes and David Hookes all there to honour him.

Nugget met the Queen of England when he lined up with the team on a Crusaders tour. In fact, one day at Windsor Castle he asked after her corgis, and the Queen was more than happy to give Nugget the full run-down.

He is a legend and I absolutely love him. He has been at my side for close to twenty years now and I cherish his support and friendship.

So with Nugget in my corner that summer how could I go wrong?

The other great partnership I started to forge that summer was with my boyhood hero, David Hookes. Hookesy and I put on some amazing partnerships during that season. In fact, I still get people in the street telling me that when news filtered through that David and I were at the crease, they would get their mates together, order a taxi and get to the ground. It was just extraordinary, two left-handers batting with total abandonment and getting away with it. If I saw that the first ball was in the right place, I would just flick it over mid-wicket into the crowd. I tried all sorts of things I wouldn't dream of trying now. I didn't know you weren't meant to bat like that in a four-day game. I didn't know those bowlers were supposed to be treated with more respect. I was an eighteen-year-old having the time of my life.

As you get older you realise that these patches don't last, but back in 1989 I was all about entertainment. I would get to 70 and pretty much start swinging from the bootlaces. I would try to hit each ball further than the one I had just faced. That's the way you think when you are a teenager; you think no-one can touch you, that you are ten foot high and bulletproof. You basically think the run is going to last forever. Of course, it never does and indeed on this occasion history shows that it didn't, but I can confidently say that I have never batted better than I did at the start of that season in 1989.

David Hookes gave me a very valuable piece of advice at that stage and it is something I have heeded ever since. After I made the double century against New South Wales, he told me to write down everything I had done the previous forty-eight hours – the food I had eaten, the time I had gone to bed, what I had for breakfast and the training I did the night before the match and the day of the game. In summary, every detail I could think of in the lead-up to playing that innings.

His theory was it would give me a reference point in the future, so that I could recall exactly how I had prepared for the best innings I had played to that point. What he was saying, in a nutshell, was get yourself a routine that works and stick to it.

And I have, for seventeen years.

Back then it helped me put together the best three months of batting I was capable of – that's what I thought, anyway.

Obviously some important people higher up agreed with me because in January, 1990, I found myself selected in the Test squad for the Sydney match against Pakistan. Geoff Marsh and David Boon were both injured and that meant the Australian selectors needed to find some replacements – and fast. When the squad was announced, my name was there, along with Tom Moody and Mike Veletta.

I had received a call from the chairman of selectors, Lawrie Sawle, a day earlier and he told me I had been picked in the squad for Sydney.

That is an amazing call to receive, I can tell you. Right from when you are a boy just out of nappies, if you are born in Australia you dream of one day wearing the baggy green cap. I did, anyway. Playing for your State is sensational but getting picked to play for your country is something else.

Cricket is a very elitist sport when you think about it. There are literally thousands, in fact hundreds of thousands, of people playing cricket on any given weekend around Australia. From that vast group, sixty-six players are fortunate enough to play Sheffield Shield (Pura Cup) cricket and then just eleven players climb to the top of the mountain and play for Australia.

That's eleven in a country of twenty million people, roughly half of them men, so the odds are eleven out of ten million.

Comparing it, for instance, with AFL football, where on a weekend in the winter 350 players are playing for sixteen clubs at the highest level, you start to understand how difficult it is for a cricketer to get a game for his country.

I didn't fully understand that back then. I was on the crest of a wave that hadn't broken yet, but in the years that followed I certainly came to fully understand just how tough it is to crack a regular berth in the national team.

When the news got out the press descended on the sports store where I was working, and there were more media waiting for me when I got home: TV cameras outside our house and the phone ringing non-stop.

My South Australian team-mates rang with messages of congratulations and good luck, as did my mates from Salisbury, work and school. People came out of the woodwork to wish me all the best. People I hadn't heard from for years, people I had even forgotten I knew, made contact. It was quite amazing. I am sure it is the same for anyone who gets picked to play for Australia. It's all great and you appreciate the good wishes from everyone, but at the same time the whole thing almost engulfs you. It's like a tornado that just picks you up and carries you away. You feel like you have suddenly become the centre of the known universe.

You haven't, of course, you have just been picked to play in a sporting team, simple as that, but at the time it takes on a life of its own and that's what I found myself in the middle of.

I was certain from the start that I wasn't going to be included in the final XI. I don't know why. Perhaps the gut instinct I spoke about earlier was there to guide me again, but I just knew I wasn't going to be a part of the action in Sydney.

Not getting a hit in the nets until after Merv Hughes had finished may have also given it away.

In the beginning I didn't give a toss. I thought back then there was plenty of time for that. Here I was with only a dozen first-class matches under my belt and suddenly a part of the Australian team being captained by the great Allan Border.

How wrong I was with that line of thinking. It would be almost eight years until I made my way back into the team and actually played a Test match. Back then I thought I had time on my side and I knew that eventually my turn would come.

I remember the press were keen for me to play. The papers love a new face and were all screaming for my inclusion. But the team needed openers. Boon and Marsh were out of the side and that meant that Moody and Veletta were going to play, and they were always going to bat one and two.

This made it a strange week, I must admit. I was part of the action, part of the big show, but in a real sense I wasn't a part of it at all. You never feel quite right when you are the twelfth man in a cricket team. It doesn't matter how nice the other players are to you, when you are carrying the drinks you may as well be the guy serving the lunch. Sure, there is a chance you will have to go out and field and if you do you need to be as switched on as every other player on the field.

But it doesn't matter how much fielding you do, how many pairs of gloves you run out, how many hits you have in the nets – you are basically not part of the playing XI.

But before that, the day I got my kit was so exciting. A massive parcel arrived – I knew immediately what was in there so I grabbed it and headed straight to my room. I couldn't wait to rip it open and pull out the Aussie jumper with the coat of arms on the front. That went straight on, as did the playing shirts that only the Australian players wore.

I would love that moment to have been filmed by a hidden camera so I could look back at the way I carried on. It must have looked hilarious – there I was in front of the mirror, dressed head to toe in this brand new stuff, thinking I was the best thing since sliced bread.

But that feeling didn't last long and as soon as I arrived in Sydney I knew wasn't going to play.

I still reckon I should have played. I don't know who shouldn't have played or what they should have done with the batting order, and I don't want to demean Mike Veletta or Tom Moody, who were both fine players and deserved their chance, but I thought then, as I think now: if you are going to bring in a young player – and when I say young I mean around twenty – you may as well play him. Otherwise leave him out altogether.

It was the last Test match of the year, there was nothing to lose and I was obviously in very good form. I sometimes wonder how different things might have been if I had been included in the side.

That said, you always feel better about being the twelfth man than the thirteenth, so I set about enjoying myself. I took to being around the Australian team like a duck to water. That week in Sydney I had a ball. I went to nightclubs, restaurants, I followed the big names like Dean Jones, Steve Waugh and Merv Hughes wherever they went and I was blown away by the way they were treated. It was like they were royalty. No-one gave a stuff who I was, basically because no-one knew who I was. So I slipped under the radar and had the time of my life.

But it was hard work, too. Bob Simpson was the coach at the time and his training sessions were the stuff of legend. Some of the fielding routines he put me through during that week were bloody hard.

Bob Simpson and I were never on the same page. I don't know whether the way I played wasn't disciplined enough for him, or I was the wrong body shape, or he thought I hadn't done enough to warrant selection. I honestly have no idea why we didn't get on, but I didn't play for Australia that summer, Test matches or one-day games, and I didn't get a look in for another eight years.

After that Test match was over, the one-day series started and I was retained in the squad, even though I wasn't selected for either of the first two matches. I was then overlooked later in the series when a batsman was needed and they drafted in Mark Waugh from New South Wales. Don't get me wrong, he was then and continued right throughout his career to be a sensational player, but I couldn't work out at the time how I could have been good enough to be selected in the side three weeks earlier.

It puzzled me that when a batsman was required – and I certainly thought I was a batsman – I was overlooked and they went with a player who wasn't even in the squad at the start of the series. He certainly hadn't made 700 first-class runs before Christmas – neither had Moody or Veletta for that matter – and yet they all played before me.

This was the start of a long and often mystifying relationship between myself and the people who chose the Australian team. But to be fair to them, in the next two seasons I didn't really give them much to think about.

FOUR
VICTORIA

One of the biggest gripes I have had with the Australian selectors over the years is that they totally discount runs made by batsmen batting in Adelaide, yet pick bowler after bowler who take wickets in Brisbane.

For fifteen years Brisbane has been a fast bowler's paradise. They make green, under-prepared pitches up there and bowlers like Carl Rackemann, John Maguire, Craig McDermott, Andy Bichel, Michael Kasprowicz and Adam Dale would take sacks of wickets every season.

That was good enough to get them picked to play cricket for Australia, which was fair enough, but when a batsman who played at the Adelaide Oval – or Bellerive, for that matter – made 1000 runs in a season, they were labelled 'flat-track bullies'.

How does that work? It seems that runs got discounted but wickets didn't.

The other thing that always puzzles me is the pitch at the SCG. For much of my playing time, it has been slow and flat and pretty comfortable to bat on. Yet none of the New South Wales batsmen are ever accused of making easy runs.

You really have to go back to Ian and Greg Chappell to find the last South Australian-born and bred batsmen who were 'long-term' Australian players, almost forty years ago. Sure, in that time we have seen David Hookes, Wayne Phillips, Greg Blewett and myself play a fair bit of Test cricket, but with respect to all of us, there hasn't been an 80-match Test player among us.

I have always thought batsmen out of Adelaide have been behind the eight ball from the start. I realised early that we needed to do a whole lot more just to break even and I was determined to break this mould.

That's why I jumped at an offer from Victoria to move across there for the 1990–91 season.

I can't count the number of people who have come up to me over the years and asked, 'Why did you go to Victoria? You'd been picked for Australia the previous season, you were flying, why the move?'

It's a fair question, but I did give it a lot of thought and I really believed I knew what I was doing.

You have to understand that in 1990, I was only twenty. I really wanted to break that line of thinking that was developing: that I was only making lots of runs on a flat wicket. I wanted to prove to everyone, and myself, that I could score runs in another state. I felt I needed to make the move to develop and enhance my game. Another enticing thing for a twenty-year-old was that Victoria was offering a lot more money. I'd be lying if I said that had no bearing on it. Sheffield Shield cricketers back then, even the best ones, were earning around $25,000 a season. I thought a little more financial security wouldn't go astray if I was going to support a family.

South Australia was not prepared to pay me any more and to be honest why should they have? David Hookes was paid the same amount as everyone else and they weren't all of a sudden going to pay me more than the skipper. Besides, I didn't want it to turn into a bidding war; it was never my intention to hold a gun to the South Australian Cricket Association's head, I think that would have been a poor way to behave.

So how did it all happen? It was a pretty amazing chain of events for a boy whose work portfolio at that stage amounted to factory hand at Holden and shop assistant at a sports store.

After the 1989–90 season I was invited to Melbourne to discuss the prospect of perhaps changing states and playing for Victoria. This was a very unusual thing in those days; players generally moved only because they couldn't get a consistent game for their home state. You rarely got a first-team player being 'poached' by another state.

The Australian Cricket Board frowned upon this practice, so the states were reluctant to actually approach anyone. The way they got around this was to get a club to make the offer. That way if the whole thing blew up, the state could effectively wash its hands of it.

I met with Bill Lawry, who was working for the Victorian Cricket Association at the time. He was afraid someone was going to see us so we met behind a tree outside the MCG. How funny is that? He said something along the lines of, 'Come over and we will help you achieve your goal to play for Australia'. It was great for me to spend five minutes with such a legend; he was so impressive and encouraging.

In the winter of 1990 I was invited to a meeting at the

Carlton Social Club. As I walked in, sitting at the head of the table was John Elliott, the legendary president of the Carlton Football Club and a great achiever in the corporate world. At that stage the Carlton football and cricket clubs were both run by the Carlton Social Club, which is why John Elliott was involving himself in the running of the cricket club.

As I sat down, Big John just looked at me and said, 'Well, what will it take you to sign'?

I was like a rabbit in the headlights. I had no idea this was where it would lead. I thought we were there to have a general chat about perhaps playing cricket for Carlton, not talking money in the first five minutes! I had no idea what to say. I certainly had no idea what I was worth and these were the days before anyone had a manager to handle these sorts of things. I just tried to think of everything I wanted. I thought there was no way they would agree to it, but I would ask for the earth anyway, and see what happened. After all, what did I have to lose? So I said I wanted a house, a car, a job, a job for my wife, and I wanted a certain amount of money over and above what I was likely to earn playing for Victoria.

I looked up the boardroom table. Sitting around John were Ian Collins, also a big hitter at Carlton and a man who would go on to run the Telstra Dome and become the president of the football club; Victorian coach Les Stillman; and the president of Carlton Cricket Club, Gary Schickerling. In fact, it is funny thinking of Elliott and Collins sitting at the same table. Many years later they became embroiled in a bitter and ugly battle for the Carlton presidency. But when I met them they got along really well.

So I finished asking for the world and waited with baited breath for Elliott to thank me for my time and tell me that my services wouldn't be required after all.

But John didn't bat an eyelid. He just looked me in the eye and said, 'Right, you ready to sign?'

I nearly fell over. I somehow managed to get out of the room without signing and jumped on a flight home. I needed to give myself some thinking time. But even while I was sitting on the plane I knew that I was going to take up the offer.

Looking back now, compared to what Sheffield Shield players are earning these days it was nothing. But to me, at twenty and just married, it was more than I could dream of earning.

The thought of testing myself in a new place, on a new ground, appealed strongly. I thought I would show the doubters that I was good enough to make runs on any surface.

Of course, the people at the Adelaide Oval were not overly impressed and I couldn't blame them. They had nurtured a young player to the point where he was playing very good first-class cricket, and they were entitled to expect him to give them plenty of service. You can imagine their reaction when they found out that I was not only moving, but I was moving to the arch-enemy. There is, of course, a strong rivalry between South Australia and Victoria.

David Hookes was publicly quite critical of the decision, which made sense; he was losing a player who had made 1000 runs the year before. It's funny to look back on his stance, given that he went on to call Melbourne his home for years and he became the coach of the Victorian cricket team.

What David said publicly could at times differ from what he

said behind closed doors, and I remember talking to him about the decision at the time. His take on it was that I had to make the call that was right for me. He obviously didn't want me to take off but at the same time he knew an offer like that wasn't going to come along again for a while. He said forget about everyone else and make the right decision for you.

That decided, all I had to do was focus on making plenty of runs for Carlton and Victoria, because both teams had been pretty ordinary the previous season.

What I wasn't ready for was how much different the dynamics of the Victorian side would be from the South Australian one I had just left.

In the South Australian team there was David Hookes and then the rest of the players. We had this one big name who pretty much ran everything and everyone else just fell in behind. As captain in those days, you were really the captain *and* the coach, and you really ran the ship. I am not sure in hindsight whether that was a good thing but that's how it was.

In Victoria there was Simon O'Donnell, who was the captain and a member of the Australian one-day team that had won the World Cup in India in 1987. He had recently overcome cancer and was loved and admired by the Australian public. He was at the time the all-rounder in the Aussie one-day side.

Then there was Dean Jones, the supremely confident, self-promoting number three who was the king of the Australian one-day side and playing very good Test cricket as well. Who could forget the day he asked Curtly Ambrose to take off his sweatband before he bowled in a day/night game at the SCG? Pure arrogance, for sure, but that's what he was like. He believed in his ability to the fullest and I admired that. He was the best batsman in the team and he wasn't captain of Victoria, even though he thought he should have been.

Jamie Siddons was also in that side. An amazingly gifted batsman, he had gone to Pakistan with the Australian team and would have played a lot more than one one-day international on that tour if he hadn't fallen ill with a terrible stomach bug. It not only wrecked his tour but knocked him around for the next twelve months. He was a captain in the making, as he went on to prove in 1995–96 when he led South Australia to its first Sheffield Shield in fifteen years.

On the bowling side there was Merv Hughes, the enforcer from the Test team who really was larger than life. He was one of the biggest names in the game and was a massive presence in the dressing room for more reasons than just his size!

Add to that names like Paul Reiffel, Damien Fleming and Tony Dodemaide and you start to understand that this was not just an extremely talented team, but one with some very strong personalities. It often resembled a volcano that was boiling away underneath the earth and could explode at any moment.

The other interesting thing was that the coach, Les Stillman, was more often than not the person adding fuel to the fire instead of being a calming influence on the players. It was a very volatile environment in which to play cricket. Les was a coach who started out with the right intentions, but just got so caught up in it that he couldn't see how badly things were developing.

It was an incredible time to be playing cricket in Victoria and it was totally different to anything I had ever experienced.

As a young player having just arrived, I wasn't significant enough to be involved in all this, but it definitely made for a strained atmosphere in which to try to fit in and play.

That said, there were some fantastic people in that side who made me feel most welcome, none more so than Merv. I loved him from the start. He was the same when he opened the bowling for Footscray as he was when he opened the bowling at the MCG on Boxing Day. He is a big man with a great big heart and was always sensational to play with.

Siddons was a champion little bloke who never changed, no matter what was going on around him. He just played and when the egos started kicking in would just roll his eyes and walk away.

Fleming, Reiffel, wicketkeeper Darren Berry and Dodemaide all became great mates. In fact, every member of the team was fine when you were one on one. There wasn't one guy there you wouldn't happily have a beer with. The problems only arose when they all came together.

Despite the dressing room unease, my first year playing for Victoria was the one in which they secured the Sheffield Shield for the first time in more than a decade. Put very talented people together in any sporting team and they will find a way to perform well, even if they don't necessarily get along too well. Sportspeople at that level are very proud people and generally they will make sure they get the job done, even if they are not totally enamoured with the bloke at the other end.

It will usually work for a period of time, but then the fabric of the thing starts to fall apart and that was what happened with Victoria in the early 1990s. We had a team good enough to win two or three Sheffield Shield titles and perhaps we would have if the leaders in the group had been more united.

My first season coincided with the building of the Great Southern Stand at the MCG, so we played nearly all our home games at the Junction Oval in St Kilda. It actually proved to be the best thing that happened to us that year. Why? Because the pitch at the Junction Oval had a nice little ridge running just short of a good length at one end. That happened to be the end Paul Reiffel bowled from all season and 'Pistol', as we called him, kept hitting it at good pace. He ended up with a pile of wickets and we dominated at home on the back of it. Siddons also had an awesome year, peeling off 1000 runs and scoring at a rate that gave us plenty of time to bowl the opposition out.

The Shield final that year was a high-quality game, and it was a match I very nearly didn't play in. About three weeks out from the final I was hit in the eye in the nets. It was a bad blow; it basically shattered my cheekbone and required major surgery to repair the damage. Now that I have lost my hair, you can see the long scar down one side of my head.

The bowler, Stephen Irvine, played at Carlton and I was batting in the nets at Princes Park, as it was called then, with just a white floppy hat on. I top-edged an attempted pull shot and it flew straight into my face.

The next thing I remember I was carted off into the football dressing rooms. As I looked up there was Carlton's towering ruckman Justin Madden looking down at me and my caved-in face. The Carlton footballers were about to start training and he was staring at me like I had three noses.

Off I went to hospital, where they had to peel the skin off my face and insert a plate after hours of surgery repairing the bones around my eye socket. My mates at the time asked why the surgeon didn't attempt to fix up my looks at the same time, but I have to say I wasn't seeing the funny side of it at all.

The incident actually changed my whole outlook on life and cricket. I remember just wanting to see again; I wasn't worried about playing any more. It's amazing how something like that can alter your priorities.

When I did come back to playing, it was the week before the Shield final against New South Wales at the MCG, and in hindsight I really shouldn't have played. There was no way I was fit enough, mentally or physically, to line up in a match of that importance.

The fitness test involved facing Reiffel in the nets and the coach and selectors had obviously told him to test me out with some short ones. He told me this was going to happen and he also told me not to worry because he would make sure he didn't hit me. Thanks, mate! I did appreciate him looking after me because I could actually hardly see, and if he hadn't been such a good mate I could have really been in trouble.

As it turned out we won the game and the Shield. I didn't contribute too much; I made ten and didn't have to bat in the second innings, which was good for me. Jamie Siddons capped off a great year with a superb second-innings century to guide us home, with my great mate Darren Berry helping him out, and helping me out at the same time because I really was in no shape to bat.

But we got there and it was a very satisfying feeling, even

though I was struggling at the time with a very sore face and some unanswered questions about how I was going to bounce back the following year.

The thing about getting hit in the face is that it has an effect somewhere in the back of your mind, a place you don't even know exists. Whereas before I didn't even consider the danger of being hit – the thought never crossed my mind – suddenly the fear would strike, like the 'yips' in golf. It was something I had no control over.

I was lucky in a way, because the final was obviously the last game of the year and I had a good five months before I had to worry about putting myself through that mental test again.

We played New South Wales at the start of the next season and I made 30 and felt pretty good. I was certainly comfortable and remember coming out of that game thinking all was well.

The next game was against South Australia and I was out for one, caught at short leg off the fast bowler Denis Hickey. That was the last hit I had in that game as Dean Jones made two big hundreds and we won easily.

Then the Victorian selectors dropped a bombshell: I was going back to the second XI to try to find some form. I couldn't believe it – I had made more than 700 runs the year before at an average of 45 and after a 30 and a miss I was being dumped. Turns out it was the best wake-up call I could have been given. I had to face up to the fact that I hadn't fully recovered from being hit in the eye and I went to work. I faced bouncer after bouncer and got my act together against short-pitch bowling.

In the second XI game that followed in Sydney I peeled off

238 against Phil Alley, Andrew Jones and Richard Stobo, all players who had played first-class cricket. It got my season right back on track. From there I went on to make 900 for the season for Victoria.

But as I was playing better, the team dynamics were getting worse. We had all this talent, we were the reigning champions and yet the whole thing was falling apart at the seams.

It probably forced me to grow up and it certainly instilled in me one of the best lessons you can learn in life, let alone professional sport. That is, you only ever concern yourself with what you can control. There was nothing I could do about the problems Les Stillman and Simon O'Donnell had with each other. All I could do was make sure I was as well prepared as I could be for every game.

Still, when you have those sorts of problems at the sharp end of an organisation, there is never a surprise when the performances start to eventually fall away. We finished out of the running just two years after winning the title. That was a disgrace when you look at the quality of the players in the Victorian side at the time.

Add Shane Warne to the names I mentioned earlier. He started playing around that time and that should have simply made a good side better. Talent-wise, it was the best first-class team I have ever seen and yet we failed to achieve half of what we should.

As for me, well, I have to admit there were times when I started to doubt the wisdom of my decision to move over from South Australia. In two years I had basically gone from next-picked to 66th-picked for the Australian team!

However, I do think I achieved my goal of proving I could bat on all surfaces. I made 900 runs the second year, but I still wasn't close to playing for Australia. The funny thing about that was at the time I never really stopped to dwell on it. I don't remember ever having a 'woe is me' attitude. I can't explain it but I was never worried about things eventually working out. I somehow just knew they would.

As I mentioned earlier, the biggest problem I had with Victoria was the in-fighting in the main team. I never had a problem with the people who worked at the Victorian Cricket Association, and the guys at Carlton were sensational.

I had an offer from Carlton at the completion of the third year for a five-year extension with a substantial increase and more responsibility. It was a very tempting proposition, but in reality, after the three years was up I couldn't get out of Victoria quick enough. The problems in the running of the Shield team had got to a stage where it was simply a miserable place to be and I thought life was too short to put up with it.

Cricket is a game and you play any game to enjoy it. It shouldn't matter whether you are playing a Test match or a game of Twister on the lounge room floor, the reason you are doing it is because it's fun.

Playing for Victoria, even though I averaged 45 there and think I played pretty well, had ceased to be fun a long time before I decided to leave. So when the general manager of the South Australian Cricket Association, Barry Gibbs, phoned me to ask how I would feel about coming home, there was never any question in my mind that the time was right.

I remember walking into Ian Collins' office at the Carlton Social Club. James Sutherland was there, too; at that time he was the accountant. I said I would need until the end of that final year to make a decision about whether to stay, as I was very unhappy with the running of the Victorian team. To their credit they were fantastic; they never put me under any pressure to sign at Carlton. In fact, they were very good to me both on and off the field for the three years I was there.

Another thing that helped make up my mind to return to Adelaide was word that Les Stillman didn't want me selected in the final two matches because he thought I was returning to South Australia. At that stage I was still going over it all in my mind, but as soon as I heard that I thought, 'That's it, I am definitely leaving, I just can't operate with this bloke'.

My last innings for Victoria was an 80 against New South Wales. I remember really working hard to get us through so we wouldn't lose the game. I was dismissed in the last half-hour and was pretty angry about getting out at that point, but Simon O'Donnell came to me and told me it was the best innings I had played for Victoria.

It was nice of him to have said that and I was happy that he and I finished on a positive note. On a personal level our last year together had been very good. There was still a lot to do with the running of the side that I didn't agree with, but as blokes we got on fine and still do.

But the horse had bolted as far as Victoria was concerned, and as soon as that last game was completed I prepared to return home and get stuck back into cricket in Adelaide.

I had viewed the turnaround of their cricket under the strong captaincy of Jamie Siddons from afar and I couldn't wait to get over there and get into it.

Had the Victorian experiment worked? Many would say no, but I argue that it toughened me up and opened my eyes to the often cold, hard, unpleasant side of playing top-level sport. Prior to that I thought everyone just got on with everyone. You are often very naive as a teenager and I drifted along in a bubble in my first years. I left Victoria a much more battle-hardened player who knew where he was headed and what he needed to do to get there.

No, I didn't have a blockbusting time playing for the Big V, but I know I wouldn't have played nearly as well for South Australia on my return without having experienced those hard years in Melbourne.

FIVE
SHIELD OF
DREAMS

I knew after the disaster that was the Sheffield Shield final in Brisbane in 1994–95 that we were going to go all the way the next season.

We had been the best team in 1994–95, I have no doubt about that, and the only reason we didn't host the final and Queensland did was because they had won games more easily. What I mean by that is, the Queenslanders played on bowling green tracks every second week and got the games finished in two and a half days.

South Australia, on the other hand, relied on spinners to get the wickets on the last two days and that meant our wins were harder to come by. Still, both states finished on 36 points.

I am sure that had that final been played in Adelaide we would have won just as comfortably as they did in Brisbane. But history shows they gave us one of the greatest five-day thumpings ever, and went on to win their first Sheffield Shield in the process. Until that time they had been the running joke of Australian sport. Their teams had been full of massive names like Greg Chappell, Jeff Thomson, Wes Hall, Majid Khan, Viv Richards, Alvin Kallicharran, Kepler Wessels,

Graeme Hick and Ian Botham, but they had never been able to climb the mountain.

Of course, now they are one of the powerhouse states in the competition but back then they hadn't won and I can't stand the fact I was part of the team that handed them their first Shield.

It was an ugly game.

The ground was full every day and the crowd was understandably hostile towards South Australia. We were on their turf and they wanted to win, badly. On the first day of the match we hit the ground for warm-ups about 8.45 a.m. (matches start early in Brisbane due to not having daylight saving), and the place was nearly full even then.

I still remember on the warm-up lap the crowd singing: 'With a knick, knack, paddywhack give a dog a bone ... South Australia, fuck off home!' And that before the game even started!

We won the toss and elected to bat, something we had done all season, and before you could blink were four for 30, with Andy Bichel, Dirk Tazelaar and Carl Rackemann splitting the top order. We clawed our way to 214, but the pitch was good and only getting better and I think we knew at stumps on the first day that we were pushing the brown stuff uphill.

I was disappointed not to get any; I had a good feeling going into the game and had always played well at the Gabba. And being four for not many was something we had avoided all season – someone in the top four had always managed to make a score and get us up to the 350-plus we needed to give the bowlers something to work with. But on this day Ben Johnson, Paul Nobes, Jamie Siddons and I were all in the dressing room in the first half-hour and we struggled from that point.

I say it was an ugly game because the feeling between the

two sides was bad from the first day.

Australian first-class cricket to that point had always been about the cricket being played on the field and the beer being drunk off the field, and really never the twain shall meet. I was brought up to believe that no matter what happened on the field, you always went in to the opposition dressing room for a beer if your team was batting. It didn't matter if you had had a stand-up row with an opposition player on the field and he had called you every name under the sun. When the day's play finished that was all forgotten and in you went.

Sheffield Shield cricket had been like that for more than a century, but not this game. We had been dismissed for bugger all and the Queenslanders were none-for-plenty at stumps on day one. You didn't have to be a historian of the game to know they were in the box seat.

But in we went to have a drink with them. I can tell you we weren't exactly feeling excited about it – there they were in a tight circle and none of them would speak to us.

I gather someone must have instructed them before the game that socialising with the opposition was out for the next five days. Anyway, we turned around and walked out and that was the last time any of us spoke to any of them for the week.

It was a fair rout; Queensland's first innings finished at 664 and we were dismissed in our second dig for 349.

Funnily enough, after the game some of their players tried to get stuff signed by our blokes and they were given very short shift. As I said, it was an ugly game.

But I reckon it was while sitting in the Brisbane Lions rooms at the Gabba after we had lost, watching our team mascot Nugget with tears streaming down his face, that the desire

started to grow for the following season. I knew we were a better team than we'd just shown and I knew the next year we
were gong to win the Shield – I don't know how, but I knew.

Good teams in sport are rare. They don't come along every day
and often they just evolve. There is not a lot of science about it.

South Australia was one of those teams.

Paul Nobes and I had returned from stints in Victoria and
we joined a line-up that was already pretty good.

Jamie Siddons was one of the best players I had seen and I
had watched him first-hand peel off 1000 runs for Victoria in
1990–91.

Greg Blewett was just starting to blossom into the fantastic
player he would become and James Brayshaw had come from
the west and was playing well.

Basically the top five batsmen were averaging around 45 or
better in first-class cricket and that is unusual.

Add to that Tim May, the best finger-spin bowler in the
country; Peter McIntyre, the second best leg-spinner in the
land; Jason Gillespie, who even then was superb; Shane
George, who was mad; and a really good wicketkeeper-bats-
man in Tim Nielsen. This was a very good side.

I knew we were going to win the Shield. It was just a matter
of when.

The pre-season after the debacle in Brisbane was hell. I have
never been that keen on pre-season training but that winter we
worked harder than ever before, doing things like one-kilome-
tre 'reps', which basically meant you had to run one kilometre,
five times, with three-minute breaks in between.

And your times weren't allowed to differ by more than

thirty seconds from your fastest time to your slowest. Try doing that! Paul Nobes, while a fine batsman, was no physical specimen and one of his times clocked in at eight minutes. You could walk faster than that.

We did triathlons, canoed down rivers in the freezing cold … you name it, we did it, but we were fit for the start of the season.

We also made a pact to play a more attacking brand of cricket.

We decided to get the fast bowlers to pitch the ball up a bit more, bring Tim May on when the ball was hard, set attacking fields and basically take our game to a new level.

It worked. At the end of the ten games we had earned the right to host the Shield final and we were going to take what we considered was rightfully ours.

But standing in the way of holding that famous Shield aloft was one of the most gripping five-day cricket matches ever.

The lead-up to the 1995–96 Sheffield Shield final against Western Australia was enormous. There was a complete buzz around town. Looking back on it, we probably got caught up too much in the hype of having the match at home. We also got caught in the jet stream of one of the most brilliant innings I have ever seen.

At this stage Adam Gilchrist was seen as an enormously talented cricketer who hadn't yet shown what he was capable of. But what he did in the first innings of that Shield final at the Adelaide Oval was staggering.

We were right in the game at stumps on day one and suddenly at stumps on day two Western Australia had declared at nine for 520 and we were two for not much. Gilchrist had single-handedly ripped the game out from underneath us!

They had put a temporary stand on the Victor Richardson Gates side of the Adelaide Oval and thank God it was there; if not we would have lost a dozen balls into Queens Park.

'Gilly' just kept belting Peter McIntyre and Tim May into the seats. He scored 189 not out, off only 187 balls, including fifteen fours and five sixes. After he passed 30 not one ball missed the middle of the bat.

The way he brought up his century – with a flat pull-shot for six into the members' seats – probably summed it all up. He'd come in when Western Australia was five for 215 and simply thrashed us.

Thing is, he's played ten hands like it since, but at that stage we hadn't seen anything like it and it sat us right back on our heels.

So instead of being able to enjoy the five days in beautiful sunshine at the Adelaide Oval, we were involved in one hell of a scrap.

In reply, Paul Nobes made 103, James Brayshaw got to 87 with the help of the tail and we managed to get past the follow-on, which was vital. I have no doubt we would have lost the game if we were made to bat again. As it was we reached 347.

The thing that probably saved us was our bowling in the second innings. We bowled superbly and put the pressure back on them, probably for the first time in the game. Jason Gillespie took four for 33, really showing what a huge talent he was, and in the process stemming the flow of runs for Western Australia, and buying us some time. The less time we had to bat in our second innings, the more likely we were to draw the final and win the Shield.

I think that's where the West Australians cost themselves the game. They stuffed about after losing early wickets and made another declaration at eight for 169, setting us 347. They should have just kept going for it because they needed the time to bowl us out on the last day (the visiting side has to win the match outright to be declared champion).

Still, the last day of the match was the most nail-biting day of cricket I've been involved in.

I was out first thing on the fifth morning – lbw to Brendon Julian for a duck – and that made it worse because I had to sit and watch all day knowing there was nothing I could do.

Our captain, Jamie Siddons, was crook – he had a block in his hip that meant he was struggling to move, let alone run. James Brayshaw had a torn thigh muscle and was lucky to pass a fitness test before the match even started. When I got out we had seven wickets left and about seven and a half hours to survive. It wasn't looking good.

I remember it was a beautiful day, the pitch was superb and about 4000 faithful fans had come hoping to see their team win the trophy for the first time since 1981. South Australian cricket fans are pretty special. They are very knowledgeable and have at times had to suffer some pretty ordinary cricket. What they got this day was one of the most pulsating days imaginable.

At one stage it looked like we weren't going to need the full amount of time: James Brayshaw and Greg Blewett were scoring at five an over and we were on track to win the match outright. Then Brayshaw hit one straight up in the air and that's really where the trouble started.

From then on we consistently lost wickets, and when Tim Nielsen was bowled with the first ball after tea, we needed to bat through the whole session with three wickets in hand.

At that stage it was too much for Paul Nobes and me: we went for a four-kilometre walk around the Torrens River to escape the tension ... and we weren't on our own. Greg Blewett jumped in his car and drove around the suburbs of Adelaide trying not to listen to the game on the radio, and four blokes started playing cards out the back of the rooms. That game lasted for hours.

The strain was almost unbearable.

After Tim May had made a 64-minute duck and Jamie Siddons had batted 166 minutes for four runs, the last pair – Peter McIntyre and Shane George – came together with an hour to go. If we lost another wicket we were cooked.

But they came to an agreement that 'Macca' would take Julian and 'Georgy' would face Brad Hogg. Somehow, they kept them out.

Over after over, ball after ball, these tailenders, numbers ten and eleven, managed to turn away two Test bowlers on a fifth-day track.

As the game went down to the wire, the crowd started to grow.

When I got back to the ground, a few more were there but it was still only about 5000. By the last couple of overs that number had swollen to 15,000. People had emptied out of the offices in town; they had arrived on the trains; been dropped off; had come on foot ... they came from everywhere. And they started to count the balls down, as one, there were 15,000 people chanting to the tune of 'Twenty bottles of beer on the wall': *'Thirty balls are left in the game, there are thirty balls left and after this there'll be twenty nine.'*

It was absolutely amazing. Every ball seemed to take an eternity.

West Australian captain Tom Moody took his time talking to his bowlers and setting his field, adding to the pressure and tension.

Then it came down to the final over: Brendon Julian to Peter McIntyre. We were six balls from glory.

That over seemed to take an hour, let me tell you.

In Julian would steam, Macca would keep him out, and the crowd would get singing: *'There are five balls left in the game, there are five balls left!'*

By this stage all the fans were on the ground. They had jumped the fence and the noise grew louder with every ball that was survived.

Julian tried going around the wicket, but still he couldn't dislodge Macca. Now we were down to the final ball.

It's an old saying, but the crowd went quiet. No-one said a word. The dressing rooms were silent; even the card game stopped for the first time in two hours.

In charged Julian to deliver a full and straight ball. Macca, as he had done for the previous hour, blocked it, and the Shield was ours.

I will never forget the scenes after it was all over.

Macca charged from the ground waving his bat around and Shane George went screaming after him. The change-rooms erupted, with people jumping on top of each other and whooping it up. Nugget, who had been in tears a year earlier, was in tears again, but this time for the right reason. It was pandemonium!

It was a great day and a sensational match. Games like that come along very rarely.

We had held out against a West Australian side that contained Tom Moody, Brendon Julian, Adam Gilchrist, Damien Martyn, Justin Langer, big Jo Angel and Brad Hogg. They had seven Test players in that side and they had thrown everything they had at us.

Unlike the previous season, we spent a good hour and a half in the West Australian team's rooms that final night, paying them the respect they were due. They were a great side and they had played a terrific match, but we'd won the Shield and I got to carry it into the team pub, The British, the next day. It was heavy, but so too were the celebrations.

SIX
FAMILY MATTERS

One of the very few downsides to playing international and first-class cricket for a long time is the significant impact it has on the people you love. Now, more than ever, players are asked to play all year round, and much of that involves interstate and overseas travel.

After seventeen years of it, I have no doubt it has taken its toll on the people I love the most, but at the same time I am very lucky because my family could not be in better shape. My wife Andrea is without doubt the best and most important person in my life. She understands the rigours of life as a touring cricketer; she is there for me when I need support; she comes with me as often as she can and she does the most amazing job of looking after our twins, Ethan and Amy.

That I am in such a good place now on the home front is not something I take for granted, because for the first ten years of my career I didn't succeed in mixing playing with my home life well at all.

This is not something unique to sportspeople, of course. Many professional people in their twenties focus on climbing the ladder – often to the detriment of those around them. I'm not saying that cricket was to blame for the break-up of my first marriage – there were many factors – but certainly the lifestyle doesn't make it easy on relationships.

But I don't want to drag up the past. I have too much respect for the people who have been close to me along the way to ever wander down that path. Andrea and I have a good understanding with my first wife and her husband, and I have a sensational bond with my two children from my first marriage, Tori and Jake.

Like most busy people, the only thing I would like is more time to see the kids. I have been extraordinarily lucky to be blessed with four magnificent children; the hard part for me is simply not getting enough time to see them.

I read once that Mick Jagger said being a rock star was okay in a parenting sense because, sure, you're away a lot, but when you get back you have a lot of free time to spend with the children. He's right – you do get slabs of time where you really can spend quality time with your kids, but the big periods of time you spend away from them really hurt.

When I was doing it tough after David Hookes died, the weeks away from Andrea and the kids were especially hard. You just want them around. You want to wake up and have them there in the morning, you want to eat breakfast with them, go to the park and read them books. I am sure other parents find this: when you are sad, the best therapy you can have is your children. They have a way of taking your mind off what you're down about and focusing your attention on them.

The way the Australian team is run now is that wives and children are encouraged to come on tours too. The hotel rooms of old are now all apartments. They have kitchens and are laid out more like a house than a hotel room. Some grounds have child-minding facilities too. Basically, families are welcome, which certainly wasn't the case when I first started playing representative cricket.

Andrea comes with me as often as she can as she knows how much I love having her and the kids with me. That said, it is hard for her to just drop everything and travel around the world with a cricket team. When we are on the road much of our time is spent either planning, playing or training, and none of those things are much fun for a young family.

England is a great place to bring them, places like New Zealand and South Africa are fine, and parts of the West Indies are sensational, but some of the countries we travel to just aren't conducive to bringing your family. India and Pakistan are not easy places to travel to with new twins. Safety and health are definitely concerns. Enough players go down with bugs of different kinds without exposing the little ones to it. So if there is a two-month tour of the subcontinent, it really isn't all that practical to have your family with you.

It can get very lonely in places like Pakistan and Sri Lanka when you spend all your time at cricket grounds and in hotel rooms for weeks on end while your family is back home. I have had nights sitting alone in hotel rooms overseas when the temptation to jump in a cab to the airport and fly home has been almost overwhelming. This is not unique to the Lehmann family. Most of the Australian players have partners and a majority of them have kids. We all miss our families desperately when they are not around and there is no way to hide from that.

Families are also a great tonic for cricketers, because the game will knock you around a bit from time to time. It doesn't matter how good a player you are; when you are going through a bad trot there's nothing better than having your family with you. I have experienced bad decisions or made mistakes on the field and have been furious. But when you walk through the door and see your wife and children, it's all forgotten. They don't care if you've had a bad day, they are just happy to see you and you are instantly happier for being around them.

I think one area I have improved in is being more understanding of Andrea's needs. She is bringing up young twins sometimes pretty much on her own, and needs all the emotional support she can get. Andrea, or 'Whitey' as I call her, is a champ, simple as that. I met her through her brother Craig, who I had known for years.

Craig and I had played with and against each other right through our junior representative days. He had come to the Cricket Academy in Adelaide and I had seen him then. Then I moved to Victoria and we caught up again. We actually became firm friends when I started playing County cricket for Yorkshire. He is a top man and we were good friends before Andrea came on the scene.

I had seen Andrea once before I met her and after that I was very keen to see her again. I knew I was travelling to Scarborough to play a game and I knew Andrea was going to be there, so I told Craig to tell her that she needed to show me around. Craig teed up our first meeting at a pub in Scarborough in the north of England where a few friends and team-mates were meeting up for drinks.

I am not sure Andrea was overly pleased at the thought of showing me around. She didn't know me from a bar of soap and I am sure she wasn't jumping out of her skin to spend a night with a cricketer from Australia. I must admit, I didn't help the situation by getting quite drunk prior to arriving at the pub, courtesy of an afternoon spent with former Aussie cricket legend David Boon.

After five minutes in this pub I was serving behind the bar, making a spectacle of myself and not impressing Andrea one little bit. She said later that she had looked at me and decided I was a typical Aussie travelling bloke: too much to say and way too keen on drinking.

Thankfully I extricated myself from behind the bar and actually sat down with Andrea and talked to her and that's when it all started. I think she realised there was more to me than she first thought and I certainly warmed to her.

At the time Andrea was working in Scarborough at the hospital – she is a registered nurse – and I was based in Leeds playing cricket for Yorkshire. I know she had concerns about my past. I had been married before and already had two children. I am not sure she thought her knight in shining armour would come in the form of an overweight cricketer with that sort of history. But she stuck with me and thank God she did.

Scarborough is ninety minutes from Leeds and we saw each other as often as we could after that. Then Andrea came out to Australia and met all the people who are important to me. She had spent a great part of her life in Australia so it was all a really good fit.

I am so glad she didn't turn around and walk out that first night in Scarborough. I tell you, if she had and I had missed out on getting to know this amazing girl, I would have hunted that Tasmanian Boon down and given it to him. Drinking with him is something I can do any old time, but a girl like Andrea only comes along once in a lifetime.

We were married in 1999. The World Cup had finished and it was the only gap in the cricket calendar. We both knew early in the picture that we would get married, but finding enough time to actually do it was another thing.

It was a big commitment for Andrea to marry me. I know she had watched her brother's relationship with his wife closely and she saw first-hand how much time Craig's wife spent on her own. The thought of marrying into that same life can't have thrilled her.

Andrea often tells the story that when we first decided to commit to each other, I told her I wasn't playing for Australia and wasn't likely to, so I wasn't going to be away much. At the time it was the truth. In 1997 I wasn't even being mentioned as a possible inclusion in the Australian team. I thought I would have another five years playing for South Australia and Yorkshire if I was good enough and that would see me out. Of course, no sooner had I said that than I found myself in both the Australian one-day and Test teams, and suddenly I was away more than I had ever been.

These were hard yards for Andrea. We were based in Adelaide at that stage, a place she had never lived in. I was spending a lot of time out of the state and country and she was living alone, surrounded by people she hardly knew. I am still amazed by how strong she was during that period, because she had every right to be pretty anxious.

But, as I said, Andrea's a champ and we managed to work our way through the early days without too many problems. We didn't have our own kids at that stage so she was able to come with me on the road more easily, something that obviously helped.

Life on the road as a professional sportsman has amazing benefits. You get paid well, you spend time in countries most of your mates have never thought of visiting and the hotels are generally top class. You also get to play a game you love on the best grounds in the world.

What I do have trouble convincing people about is that the novelty of the lifestyle wears off after a while. The playing is never a problem, but airport lounges, team buses and hotel rooms are no substitute for spending time in your own home with your wife and children. I look at someone like Steve Waugh and wonder how he coped so well when he did it for close to twenty years. But that's the life we lead and you'll never hear me complain about playing cricket for my State or country.

I am unique in the fact that a member of my family plays cricket for another country. Craig has played plenty of Test and one-day cricket for England in the past decade. He is such a good mate that we have bought adjoining blocks of land in the same subdivision in the eastern suburbs of Adelaide.

Craig plans to settle in South Australia with his family when he retires from cricket and it will be amazing to have them literally living next door. We didn't plan on living so close to each other. The blocks came up for sale and when we told him we were going to buy one he said he wanted in. On the day of the auction our respective blocks of choice were actually at separate ends of the lot, but as the blocks were knocked down one by one we ended up with adjoining pieces of land.

Andrea is frightened of the day we live next to each other as I really enjoy a sip and so does Craig ... and one of my favourite pubs in the world, the Edinburgh, is within walking distance. My argument that it's a good thing we can walk there and walk home seems to be falling on deaf ears.

I am not sure if brothers-in-law have ever played Test cricket against each other before, but I absolutely loved playing at that level against Craig. The Test series against England in Australia in 2002–03 tested that love a little as he got me out twice, and the first instance was in Adelaide at my 'home' Test.

Andrea wasn't at all impressed. There I was trying to establish myself as a player at that level and her brother kept getting me out. On the first occasion she didn't speak to him for a few days – her own brother! But then she had to get used to it as he got me out again in Perth. The whole experience has given us and our family many laughs, and I'm sure it will bring much to look back on when we are retired.

At the Test in Adelaide, Craig came and spent some time at our house beforehand, which was fantastic. Funnily enough, when we do catch up we rarely talk about cricket, probably because we get asked about the game constantly. When we get together we talk about everything else.

He obviously went back to the team hotel on the eve of the game and the next time I saw him was when he came out to bat in England's first innings. When he arrived at the crease I was fielding at short leg because Shane Warne was bowling, and I noticed straightaway that something was different about his look. I couldn't work out what it was. But something was different. Then, after a couple of overs I finally realised what it was. The bastard had stolen my new batting shoes from my house and was wearing them in a Test match!

I had just received some equipment from Nike, my long-term footwear supplier, and I had made the mistake of showing Craig some of it when he was staying with us. He obviously liked what he had seen. The boys were roaring; 'Warnie' and Gilly thought it was hilarious and didn't hesitate to rub it in, saying, 'Let's not make it *too* comfortable for him out here' and 'On your feet in close there, Boof'.

I wondered how I was going to tell George Lawler from Nike that I needed a new pair of batting spikes two weeks after he had given me a pair. How could I explain that an England player had pinched them from my house? I later found out that Andrea had told him to help himself, something she neglected to tell me. They say blood's thicker!

So Andrea's family have become a very important part of our lives. Her other brother, Andrew, sister-in-law Angela and their boys live in Victoria and we love spending time with them when we can. I have been very lucky to marry into a family that has accepted me, Jake and Tori completely, and I have always loved them for it.

I should also mention the love and continued support I receive from my own family. My mum is a magnificent lady. She now lives in Halls Gap in Victoria, where she and her husband own the Lakeside Caravan Park. For years she did everything for me. She cooked, cleaned, took me to and from sporting venues, helped me with schoolwork – she basically did the lot. I thought that was what all mums did, but now when I look back I realise what she provided me with was above and beyond.

When I started playing junior cricket she was the mum who would score for the team, the job no-one wanted. She would make dinners at the club and spend hours making sure everything was spotless. She knew which ground I had to be at, when, and what gear I had to be wearing. This was a good thing because at fourteen I had no idea about anything. She really gave up a lot to be there for me.

Her husband, Dennis, who she met later, is a brilliant man and they are always there for us when we need support, advice or help. As grandparents they have been invaluable. They love having the kids and the kids love being with them, which comes as no surprise given the way Mum brought me up.

My father has also always supported me, through the good times and the bad. While we don't talk every day, I suppose we get the message across in a typically Australian father-and-son way. He has never been one to interfere. He lets me go about living my life and has never waded in with his two bob's worth about how I am doing it. That is something I have always loved about him. That's not to say he doesn't care, because I know he does, deeply. But he has always taken the view that this is my life and career and it is up to me to make it work.

He has had a long and tough career in the South Australian police force and I suppose that has given him a very realistic view on life and how to go about it. My father was the officer who arrested Terry Jenner nearly thirty years ago when he fell foul of the law. I firmly believe police officers, through their consistent exposure to the 'other' side of life, have to develop a pretty thick skin, a tough exterior. But you don't have to scratch too hard to get through that with Dad, and his strength has always been something I have admired.

My other main support is the amazing group of close friends that I have. Craig 'Struds' Strudwick, Peter McIntyre and Greg Blewett are really loyal mates that I have spent many great times with. Craig and Peter are actually godparents to our children, as we are to theirs. We've played lots of cricket together, had many a late night, lots of laughs and they have been there for me through some tough times. They have also helped Andrea and the kids out enormously when I've been away.

I have found that, as you get older, family and close friends start meaning more and more to you, and I ring the people I love as often as I can, even if I really have nothing to say. Another thing you start to think about when you work your way into your mid-thirties as a cricketer is that your career is going to end at some stage. Instead of dreading that moment, I can't wait for it. I have no idea what I will do when I stop playing professional cricket, but I know I will have the most amazing group of people around me to help in whatever I decide to undertake. They are a constant through the maze of this slightly weird life and I can't thank them enough for the never-ending love and support they continue to give me.

SEVEN
HAPPY
YORKSHIRE
DAYS

The summer of 1997 was my first year at Yorkshire Cricket Club and one which for many reasons was going to change my life forever. It was a time that would change me from a person I didn't like very much, into one who was truly happy and proud of his achievements both on and off the field.

I say this because there were aspects of my life that were not the way I wanted them to be. On a professional level, I thought my international career was over, and I felt this was due to a lack of opportunity. I had played only a handful of one-day international games and it didn't look like I was going to get any more. This was extremely frustrating, particularly as I was continually making runs for South Australia. I still think that I was in the best form of my career then, and I've often wondered what I might have achieved, given more guidance and mentoring along the way.

I felt disillusioned with many things at the time but little did I know that with a couple of phone calls and a couple of selections soon going my way, I would be heading to Yorkshire and the most famous cricket club in the world.

On a personal level, I realised that I was in an unhappy marriage. We had two wonderful children, Jake and Tori, who were the true blessing to come out of the marriage, and they made the inevitable decision to leave a very difficult one.

One thing I learnt from this period is that if you are truly happy in whatever you do, it reflects in your relationships with your children and the people around you in a more positive way. And as I see how well things have turned out for everyone now, I feel that my decisions were the right ones.

Playing for Yorkshire came about thanks to my manager at the time, still a very good friend, Terry Davies. Terry, a Welshman, was a County player at Glamorgan in the mid-1980s. Welsh people, I have found, have a great sense of humour, buzz around all day and can't seem to stop. Multiply this by a hundred and you have Terry.

I had always thought that cricket in the UK was not up to the standard I was used to playing – Sheffield Shield cricket is the toughest domestic competition in the world – but I decided I had nothing to lose. With my international career looking shaky and with a real need for something new, I made the decision to see it as a challenge and just go for it. I was about to find out that the County system is a lot better than people think, and is one of the most enjoyable experiences you could imagine as a cricketer.

I think it is a must for young players to go and play County cricket, if given the opportunity. The overseas player has to endure more pressures – of being the man expected by the club and the fans to win games day in, day out; of continuing to improve himself as a player, leader and mentor to the young players – which is great for personal development. This is a part of the job that I love doing.

When Terry and I initially tested the waters on the County scene, the first offer actually came from Hampshire, as a reserve player should Matthew Hayden be picked for Australia in the upcoming Ashes Tour.

In the meantime, we started negotiations with Yorkshire. They were looking for an overseas player to replace Michael Bevan, who had been selected in the Ashes squad. It was to be for one year. I was keen to go, but when I went to notify Yorkshire of my decision I was informed they had already signed Michael Slater, who was not in the Australian Test team at the time.

I was very disappointed; I hadn't realised they were talking to both of us, which at that time I considered unprofessional. At that point it looked like I would be signing with Hampshire, as Hayden was seen as an almost certain selection for the Ashes tour. But a week is a long time in sport, and to everyone's surprise, Hayden was dropped and replaced by Slater. Suddenly, Yorkshire were on the phone wanting me to sign, and the rest is history.

As well as providing vast experience, County cricket provides a lucrative income for overseas players during their off-season. A cricketer's career is short and, depending on selection, form and injuries, playing overseas can bring some stability to an unpredictable income.

After signing I realised the enormity of the task, in that the club had not won the County Championship since 1968. They had finished third the season before I arrived, and fully expected to continue to rise, hopefully ending their championship drought.

My first experience of Yorkshire as a team was a video of the previous season sent to me by the club. First impressions were of a side that played with enthusiasm and that possessed plenty of skill, and this proved correct. In fact, Yorkshire had plenty of stars in English players like Darren Gough, Craig White, Chris Silverwood and Michael Vaughan. But also on the video was a legendary story that intrigued me. It didn't concern the Yorkshire Ripper, but rather the Yorkshire Snipper!

As I would find out, the snipper was a prime example of the larrikin culture that completes the picture of the Yorkshire cricket team; a bunch of practical jokers with a wit and sense of humour I'd never experienced before. The snipper has been snipping jocks, socks and ties of players for ten years, and is still at large.

My first taste of the snipper came during my first game at Headingley, our home ground. After the day's play, I had a shower and as I put my jocks on, lo and behold they flew up to my waist – the crutch had been snipped out. As you can imagine, the whole dressing room was in stitches. I don't think the guys knew how I would take it, but I'm sure the snipper must have been relieved to see that I could take a joke. Unfortunately, my amusement at the whole ordeal led to me becoming a regular target, and the snipper has cost me a lot of money in new jocks and socks over the years.

All the guys have vehemently denied being the snipper whenever suspicion has fallen on them and essentially nobody trusts anyone in this affair. I have my suspicions, but it remains one of Yorkshire's great mysteries. Despite being a prime victim, I do think the snipper has helped create an amazing team-building exercise. When we have a really bad day on the field and moods are low, to discover someone had been 'snipped' always brings the house down.

Of course, what goes around comes around, and Anthony

McGrath, or 'Gripper' as we call him, knows all about this. He is a king of practical jokes and has a remarkable ability to lie straight to your face as he denies all. That's one of the reasons he is on my list as the possible snipper. He's been known to regularly remove people's car aerials just before we set off on a long journey to another County ground. Travel can be pretty boring without any music.

Bananas in the exhaust pipe is another favourite trick of his, not to mention advertising our cars in the paper. Practical jokes at Yorkshire take on such amazing dimensions that one night when McGrath's car had actually been stolen, he spent many unnecessary hours trying to ascertain which one of us had taken it!

The famous Headingley Cricket Ground is the home of Yorkshire Cricket Club. It is in the city of Leeds, which is where my family and I live when we are over there. My first recollection of Leeds was amazement at how old the place is, and yet it's a very modern, happening place, bustling with business and industry. Just a short drive out of Leeds brings lush, green countryside, and fresh air – something you wouldn't necessarily expect in a small county, given its population.

Yorkshire people are hospitable, generous to a fault and they have a brilliant, dry humour. Add to that the broad accent that took me some time to understand, but which makes their one-liners even funnier. They have a strong sense of pride, they love their sport and expect their sporting teams to win every game. Whether it is the cricket side, Leeds United soccer team, Leeds Rhinos, the rugby league team, or the Leeds Tykes, the rugby union side, if they don't win the supporters want some answers. Let me tell you, you have to have thick skin on the days when you are not playing well, but all in all I guess you could say the fans are hard but fair and they always show great pleasure at a win. With my on-field success over the years, I have been really touched at how the Yorkshire crowds have welcomed and accepted me as one of their own.

My first game for Yorkshire was against Lancashire at Old Trafford in Manchester, in what was the premier competition of the year, the Benson and Hedges title. Before all games, I like to go out on the ground before anyone gets out there for the warm-up, to look at the wicket, visualise what I am going to do and get a feel for the wicket and the ground.

On this day I was out there playing a few practice shots and seeing the flattest wicket of all time. I was thinking, 'I'm going to make plenty today and make a real impression.' That was until captain David Byas came over. After a brief discussion about how we would bat first if we won the toss, he informed me that I was twelfth man. 'Pardon?' I couldn't believe it.

'Twelfth man,' he repeated, his decision based on the fact that I had just arrived and had not played for the past month – the time between the end of the Aussie season and the start of theirs.

I remember thinking, 'Geez, you pay a guy a lot of money to come a long way and then don't even play him'. But I decided to be the best twelfth man they had ever had. I was determined to make an impression somehow. The story of my first game has now become a standing joke at Yorkshire, and when Dave and I get together for a drink we still have a laugh about it.

As twelfth man in Australia it is common practice to do extra fitness work before the game. And that's how I first found out about the intense rivalry between Lancashire and Yorkshire. I was on the ground before the game doing my running, and have never heard a crowd give me so much shit as the Lancashire crowd did that day.

There I was, first game, a new face and they were singing, '*You fat bastard, you fat bastard, who ate all the pies?*' I couldn't help but laugh – a lot, actually – and it spurred me on to work harder. It was then that Gavin Hamilton told me the history between the counties, and that the most important thing for the whole year was to beat Lancashire in every game. If we did that, it had been a good year, regardless of where we finished in the championship. Well, on this occasion, we beat Lancs convincingly, we had a great game and I couldn't wait to strap on the pads.

Yorkshire has seen its fair share of cricketing legends – Geoffrey Boycott, Fred Truman and Ray Illingworth to name just three. I have been fortunate to play with some of the modern heroes. One of the more successful players in recent years, and one of the best fast bowlers, is Darren Gough.

When I first met Darren, he was the premier fast bowler playing for England, and the thing that impressed me most was his fighting spirit. He has a never-say-die attitude and therefore is one player you always want in your side when you are in trouble. I admire his pride in both the England and Yorkshire sides and his desire to always play well, regardless of how the team is going. I think the English crowds know this and they like him a lot. He never gives up, despite having endured some tough times with England. I know he always hoped to win something with Yorkshire and I think when we finally won the championship in 2001 he realised one of his dreams. I imagine only winning the Ashes would top this, but he probably won't be given another chance to do so, particularly with the way England play against Australia. They won't get the Ashes back for a while yet, and by then, I imagine 'Goughie' will have retired.

Another player I admired enormously was David Byas, Yorkshire's captain for my first four years. David was a farmer from a little Yorkshire village called Kilham. Boy, did this bloke have a strong handshake; he nearly broke my hand the first time we met.

Despite being the oldest player in the team, David was always one of our fittest blokes. It wasn't surprising when you considered that throughout his career, he not only played cricket, but whenever we were home or had a home game, he was always up at 5 a.m. doing a few hours in the fields on the tractor. Then he'd come to training or for the game. We all marvelled at how he would fit everything in, yet he never seemed to consider it a tough road and never complained. David was a good player, one who I think could have played for England, and one of the hardest hitters of the ball I have seen. He was a captain who believed in strong discipline, he never ducked an issue and he met all problems head on.

His authoritarian ways sometimes caused problems among the boys, and I have to say I would have approached some things differently. That's not to say that I don't expect full commitment, as anyone who has played under me will tell you, but I expect players to take some responsibility for their own approach and ensure they do their absolute best for their team-mates. But we all knew what David expected, he was always consistent, and in my view he was one of the fairest blokes to play under.

Craig White, now my brother-in-law, is a Yorkshire player Australians will know. I met 'Chalks', as he is known, in Victoria, where he played a couple of first-class games as a young bloke in the early 1990s and had even been selected in the Australian Under-19 team. Being an all-rounder, Craig has an amazing talent to change a game with the bat or ball.

After marrying Liz, an English girl, Chalks made the difficult decision to live in England full time and take up a first-class career with Yorkshire. Of course, back then he didn't know that he would later be selected to play for England, and that decision brought a lot of flak, as it did for Alan Mullally and Martin McCague, who made the same choice. But I admire them because they chose to take the chance given to them and play at the highest level. Let's face it, playing for a country at Test level is an amazing achievement and an opportunity you don't want to regret turning down.

One of the biggest thrills during my time at Yorkshire was at 12.13 p.m. on 24 August 2001, when David Byas took a catch off my bowling that clinched the County Championship title for Yorkshire for the first time in thirty-three years. We had won!

We were playing at one of our home grounds, Scarborough, which is a place I hold dear as it is where I met Andrea. So for me it was fitting that it should be here that the long-awaited title win came to fruition. The ground is small and surrounded by houses, and it was packed that day. It felt like there were 40,000 people cheering us on; in reality the ground only holds about 12,000, but the atmosphere was extraordinary.

I will never forget that sense of relief and the elation on not only the players' faces, but also those of our faithful fans.

They'd been waiting a long time. You could see how much it meant to Byas, and the coach who had guided us there, Wayne Clark. That year was his first at Yorkshire and Wayne had somehow managed to unite a side that had always had the potential to win, but had never delivered. Well, this year we sure brought it home. David and Wayne worked so well together to shape a team that believed in itself.

We went on to play some of the best cricket we played in my time there, with a new, positive attitude we had been missing in previous years. Wayne was an inspirational coach. He drove me to excellence that year on the field, challenging me to produce more, day in, day out, and never to be satisfied with what I had achieved already. He made me focus on getting bigger scores and concentrating on staying in to make a difference, rather than playing silly shots and getting myself out half the time.

After all the presentations and media were done, as a team we shared some of the most special moments I have experienced in the game. We sat in the change-rooms for the next four hours, had one or two beers and a few champers, and Wayne asked each of us to describe our feelings and what it meant to win the title. There were tears and a lot of them came from yours truly! Personally, I'd had a really good year and for it to end this way, well, it just made everything perfect. I remember telling these guys how much they meant to me, how they had rejuvenated my love for the game, and how Yorkshire was a home away from home because of their friendship.

We went out that night and I talked the guys into doing what we do in Australia when we win – wear your cap out and be proud. People bought us drinks all night and I can honestly say I don't remember much more to write after that.

In 2002 I had the honour of being appointed captain of the most famous cricket club in the world. I was the first overseas player to captain Yorkshire. Little did I know that it would prove to be so difficult. Where in the previous year luck had smiled upon us, this year whatever could go wrong did. We didn't play well. The weather was bad just when we needed it to hold up, and we couldn't seem to get runs or wickets, no matter how hard we tried. Many guys just seemed to be on a bad run and couldn't turn it around.

Off the field there were also plenty of issues. The club was in debt, an investigation into alleged embezzlement was taking place, and the managerial team was about to be changed completely.

I was absent on international duty for Australia for about eight weeks of the season and that didn't help. While I still made runs – in fact, it was one of my best years on that front – my role as captain felt a little disjointed when I wasn't there, knowing my team was struggling was hard. The end result saw us being relegated to second division and you can imagine the flak we got for that – from champions to wooden spooners in one season.

I was given some of the blame in the media and from some of the fans. While I had no excuses, I still felt disappointed because I had always given my all for the team and club, and this year was no different. I had tried my best, but people saw my captaincy as more lenient than that of David Byas, and some felt this was the sole reason we went down. This isn't entirely true. People who have played under me will tell you I have been known on occasion to 'go off' in the dressing room after bad performances. But certainly I do allow players some freedom to play their own game and to learn from their own mistakes.

That season we did win the Natwest one-day competition, which made us the best one-day team, but this attracted hardly any recognition in Yorkshire; people put more focus on our lack of form in the championship competition. To this day I regard it as a privilege to have captained the Yorkshire team. I know the guys in that side tried hard for me and I know it hurt them just as much as it did me that we went down. But I say to them they should be proud of bringing home two trophies in two years, because that's not a regular occurrence in Yorkshire and is something that should be recognised.

At times the County system can be conducive to dull and boring play, and this is because of the points system it adheres to. It's a concern when a team gets 20 points for winning a game, but they could also get 12 points just for drawing. Many teams won't push for a win and risk losing outright, thus losing the large number of points earned for a draw. Similarly, if Yorkshire makes 199 runs in the first innings, and the opposition is none for 400 declared, then in Yorkshire's second innings it knocks up 500 and bowls the opposition out for 120, who should win all the points? Surely the winning team. But in the current County system Yorkshire would receive 12 points for winning. And with the bonus point system coming into play, the losing team receives five points for batting and three for bowling.

The winning side really doesn't finish much ahead of the losing team. It is not only frustrating to play under such a system, but it also breeds a more cautious style of cricket, which might explain why England hasn't won the Ashes in twenty years.

I feel the whole Yorkshire experience has been a godsend for my personal cricket development. As the overseas player, I became aware early that ultimately I was being paid damn good money to win games and perform well every day. But it also brought back to me the joy and fun of playing cricket and gave me a renewed sense of purpose and the opportunity to make a real difference to the club as a whole. You can't do things like that and achieve the results that I have if you are not surrounded and supported by some incredibly good people on and off the field. I have made friends that will last a lifetime.

EIGHT
THE
BAGGY
GREEN

In the early 1990s there wasn't much made of the baggy green cap and what it symbolised. Steve Waugh hadn't worn his enough to get it as ragged and as fabled as it was in the end. Back then he was just another member of the team.

You received one whether you played in the team or not. If you were picked on an England tour it was handed to you before you left Australia. Back in the 1940s and 1950s, baggy greens were given out for every tour, with the destination and the year embroidered underneath the emblem. Sir Donald Bradman ended up with quite a few, hence the number of his caps that have come up for auction over the years.

But now that's all changed. Now you only receive a cap when you actually play in the XI. It doesn't matter how old it gets, how much alcohol has been spilt on it, how many times it's been worn in the blistering heat and how much sweat has been poured into it. You get one and that's it. And that's the way it should be.

There was never a ceremony at the handover of the cap, either. When I was first picked to play for Australia I received mine in the post.

Nowadays a past player presents the cap to the debutant and says a few words. It has become a wonderful tradition, one that I hope will carry on for many years.

The glorification of the baggy green really started to take shape with Steve Waugh at the helm of the Australian team. Steve always believed in the cap and what it meant to wear it. I reckon it was a New South Wales thing as much as anything else: the players representing New South Wales have always had 'true to the blue' as their motto and the cap has always been a serious part of their culture.

Steve brought that into the Australian arena and in the process made us all aware of how special and sacred the baggy green was.

People are sometimes critical of the condition players' caps get in, especially Steve's, which in the end was very tatty. Critics claimed his cap became almost unrecognisable and wasn't fit to be worn on the field by the Australian captain. I can understand the argument, but what they don't perhaps realise is that he wore that hat for his whole career, and an extremely good career it was too. That cap was soaked with the blood, sweat and tears of every Test match he ever played.

Cricketers seem to be superstitious people; in Steve's mind to change his cap would not have been right and a 'right mind' is very important to a professional cricketer. I think it's brilliant that he wore it right from the beginning to the end. Of course, 'Tugga' eventually had it repaired by Albion, the original hat makers that produce the baggy greens. They put new felt over the peak and tweaked it here and there and it came up pretty well.

There is no doubt the baggy green cap, along with perhaps the Wallaby jersey, is the most coveted and recognised sporting symbol in Australia and I think that is great. My one and only baggy green came with the rest of my gear in 1989. As I was the twelfth man for that Pakistan Test I didn't get to wear it – not officially anyway.

The next time I wore it, and this time it was official, was eight years later in Bangalore in northern India. I had been part of the Australian one-day team for some time and my inclusion in that side had come on the back of some big seasons with South Australia, so I got the feeling I wasn't far away from playing a Test match.

I certainly felt that if it was a middle-order batsman the selectors needed, I was going to be the player. After the twenty-four months I'd had with the bat, not only for South Australia but Yorkshire and the Aussie one-day team, if I had been overlooked for someone else I would have been filthy.

I also knew I wasn't far away because when the teams were picked for the tour of India in early 1998, I was included in both the one-day and Test squads and I was one of only seven batsmen. You didn't have to be sending rockets skywards to know that if anyone got injured or lost form, I was the next man in.

The team that went to India under Mark Taylor was very settled. They had beaten England in England the winter before, then comprehensively dealt with New Zealand and South Africa in Australia.

It's fair to say that positions in the team were reasonably hard to come by and I went to India concentrating solely on the one-day series. In a three-Test series, the selectors were highly unlikely to make a change and you never wished any of your mates to get injured. However, when you are the only spare batsman you always have the thought in the back of your mind, 'If someone falls over, I'm in!'

That is exactly what happened. We lost the first two Tests and during the Second Steve Waugh injured his groin. Given that the Second and Third Tests were scheduled about three days apart, it was going to be pretty tough for him to come up in time.

I had actually brought the baggy green cap I had been given in 1989. It had been lying in a bag at home all that time and now that I was a part of a Test squad again I had to dig it out.

On the morning of the game, when I knew I was in the side, I handed over my eight-year-old baggy green to Steve Waugh, the player I replaced in the team, for him to hand it back to me. It was as if it was mine but wasn't really mine all that time.

It was great to have it firmly on my head for the first time and feel like it really belonged, but my emotions were mixed. Here I was, picked to play a Test match for my country; I should have been over the moon and in a lot of ways I was. But I felt for Steve; nobody likes getting picked when they come in for an injured player. It feels like you are there by default. The other thing that felt strange was making my debut on the other side of the world. My great mate Greg Blewett had made his debut at the Adelaide Oval in front of his family and friends, and here I was in the middle of northern India.

So while I was pumped to finally reach a goal I had dreamed of since I was six years old, it did feel a little surreal. Those initial feelings lasted about five minutes, though, because I had a job to do and that was to play as well as I could over the next five days.

Everyone in and around the team was really supportive. Mark Taylor spoke quietly to me, saying that I had earned this chance, to relax and enjoy the experience. He reminded me that I had played a lot of cricket up to that point and, while it was a Test match, it was really just another game of cricket.

Looking back, I had been part of the furniture for a good twelve months prior to playing in that Test, so I felt very comfortable in the rooms and around the team. It was certainly much easier for a 28-year-old who was already playing in the one-day team to debut than a guy who was, say, twenty-three and a surprise selection.

We fielded first, which was a blessing for me; because I was so nervous, having the chance to walk on to the ground with the cap on as part of the XI, without the immediate pressure of batting was something of a relief. Going out on to the oval, wearing the baggy green as part of an official Australian Test team, is a feeling I will never forget.

As we hit the ground I paused and looked around, hoping it would sink in. I had goose bumps on my arms and legs. I had made it and no-one could ever take that away from me.

The really cool part of that first day was that I took a catch and a wicket before I was even required to wield the willow. One of the great things Taylor would do as captain was put the first-gamers straight into the firing line. I was sent in to silly mid-off as soon as the spinners came on and I was tossed the ball in the middle session.

I had been only a part-time bowler for South Australia but Mark knew that the best way to calm a new player was to get him involved in the game. To have taken a catch and a wicket before having to make a run was wild. My First Test wicket was a good one too: Mohammad Azharuddin, caught by Ian Healy when he top-edged a sweep. I'm sure that, by the time I am a grandfather, that story will have changed to a sharp

turning off-break that took the outside edge of the Indian skipper's bat!

That first day really helped to take the edge off the first-
game nerves. At stumps we were in a very good position and
I'd had a very enjoyable first day with the Aussie Test team.
My first innings couldn't come around quick enough.

Another great thing about that first day was watching the
little master, Sachin Tendulkar, peel off a century. I was fielding around the bat a fair bit and got to see up close just how he
operated. The time he seemed to have to do everything was
amazing and he hit the ball so hard. I have always enjoyed
watching great players do their thing and to have the best seat
in the house in your first match while watching the best player
India has ever produced make a century was a thrill.

We bowled India out for 424 and I was down to bat at number five. That's the way the Australian team did it back then
and it is pretty much the same formula now. If a batsman
comes out of the side through injury, the replacement bats in
the same spot, so as not to disrupt the rest of the batting order.
It suited me fine as I had spent much of my first-class cricket
career batting in the middle-order.

Strangely, I didn't feel nervous at all. I had had a good
night's sleep. I arrived at the ground very relaxed, the warm-up
was normal and the whole thing just felt comfortable. Even
when I was waiting to bat I didn't feel tight. Waiting to bat for
the first time in Test cricket, you would think you'd be really
toey, but I wasn't. I think the venue had a bit to do with it.
Bangalore is a quiet, easygoing place and the crowd was very
subdued. The Indians had already won the series, so much of
the sting had gone out of the match. If the game had been

played at, say, the Adelaide Oval, I think I would have felt much more tense, but that day at Bangalore I felt like I do now before any innings: on edge with anticipation, but very comfortable and confident to roll with that anticipation.

When the wicket fell and it was my turn to go in, I put my gear on and made my way to the crease. Mark Waugh was already out there, on the way to making his highest Test score of 153 not out, and he was always a great bloke to bat with, very relaxed and elegant at the crease.

I remember coming in at tea after batting for about half an hour. I had made about 20 and in the process had come down the wicket and hit Harbhajan Singh through the covers for a couple of boundaries. As we were taking our gear off in the rooms, Mark looked over to me and asked whether I had played one or a hundred Test matches. He couldn't believe how calm I had been and, in hindsight, I couldn't either. It just all felt good.

I went on to make 52 and we set up a big first-innings lead. Mark and I put on 106 and it was nice to bat for a long time with a player of his skill.

We then bowled India out cheaply in the second innings and reached the target with the loss of just two wickets. Mark Taylor made 100 in the second innings and we never looked like losing. So that was one Test for one win and a half-century – life was great.

But I was under no illusions as to my spot in the side. The team was heading to Pakistan later in the year and Steve Waugh was always coming straight back in. I was just hoping that I could hang on to my position as the spare batsman. The team for Pakistan did not include Greg Blewett, as Justin

Langer had come into the side for him, but Blewett's departure didn't really affect my chances as he was an opener, so I still thought I was going to be watching on.

As it got closer, I felt confident about the series in Pakistan as I had been playing for Yorkshire in the County Championship and my form had been good. I knew I was ripe to grab any opportunity that came my way and, after a chance discussion with Steve Waugh, I realised that chance might come sooner than I had thought.

Steve was vice-captain of the team at that stage and he came up to me during the warm-up game which I had been left out of. He asked how I was feeling, and I told him I felt good, not that it was going to make any difference because it didn't look like I was going to play.

Steve didn't say much and he didn't have to – the look he gave me said it all. It made it clear to me that I was a very good chance to play and that was enough for me; I started to get my head around batting for Australia in the First Test.

It turned out that while Ricky Ponting was selected to tour, he was the batsman the selectors had down to miss out, and I was always going to play in the first game – something nobody had bothered to tell me until my chat with Tugga.

The First Test against Pakistan was a good one for me: I made 98 and batted as well as I had for a long time, eventually getting bowled around my legs trying to sweep Mohammed Hussain for a four attempting to bring up my century.

I remember just looking around at the broken stumps in dis-belief. The thought of getting out had never crossed my mind; I knew I was going to get 100 and I knew I was going to get plenty more, that's how good I felt at the crease. My dismissal was a bolt out of the blue and I still couldn't believe it as I took my gear off in the rooms.

Still, as I always say, it's better to get 90 than nine and I'd made my second half-century in as many Test matches, which made me feel like I belonged at that level.

We then played a second tour match and this time I peeled off two hundreds. I had basically reached three hundreds in a row – some going at international level – and I was extremely confident heading into the Second Test.

That confidence, however, was shattered when I pulled up very sore after the second innings of that Tour match. I'd retired hurt on an even 100, to go with 103, but was unable to field after straining my groin. As the days wore on it became clear to me that I wasn't going to be fit for the Test.

Can you believe it? After waiting in the wings for years I was in form, guaranteed to play and suddenly I was injured. I'd rarely been injured during my whole career. I will always confess to not being the fittest man in the squad, but injury was something I had somehow always managed to avoid.

Still, missing that Test wasn't all bad; I did get to sit back and watch Mark Taylor make 334 to equal the all-time record set by an Australian player – Sir Donald Bradman. Matt Hayden, of course, topped both with his 380 against Zimbabwe in 2003–04.

The pitch at Peshawar was very flat and Pakistan in its wisdom had loaded its attack with fast bowlers, including a new kid called Shoaib Akhtar.

Going into that match, 'Tubby' (Mark) hadn't been hitting the ball all that well, and when he opened for us his first 30 were as scratchy as you have ever seen. He looked like getting out every ball until the Pakistan bowlers started trying to bounce him out. It didn't matter how badly out of form Tubby got, he could always play the pull and hook shots, and these blokes bowled him back into form.

They had three men back on the fence at one stage and he was just hitting the ball through and over them. As soon as they started banging them in he was a different player; he didn't look like getting out, and in actual fact he never did, as he declared overnight. The way he was playing he would have still been there the following week. He took the attack apart and I sat in the best armchair on the players' balcony and watched it all unfold.

Mark closing his innings has become one of the most talked-about gestures of that era. He could have batted on the next day and surpassed the Don's total, but his selfless decision was based purely on a desire to win the game. To bat on would have chewed up time in the game and we didn't have much time as it was. That's how he was; he just wanted to win every game he played in and that's what made him such a great captain.

I'm sure he desperately tried to get past Sir Donald the night before. He had one ball left to do it and he tried to get the single, but he simply couldn't get the ball past Ijaz Ahmed.

I honestly thought he was going to bat on the next day and I think the rest of the players did too, but once he had made his decision we all just got on with it. It was only when we returned to Australia that we realised he had become a saint of sorts, for declaring when he was on 334. Even the prime minister waded into it, announcing it as a great selfless gesture.

I was back in the side for the Third Test in Karachi. I made three and 26 and that was the end of the tour. I'd made 127 runs from three hands and had, I thought, shown enough to suggest I was worth persevering with in the middle order for the Ashes series in Australia against England in 1998–99.

So when it came time to announce the team for the First Test in Brisbane, you can imagine my shock when I wasn't in the starting XI. In fact, I wasn't even in the squad. I had no inkling at all that I wasn't going to play in that game – I never considered I might be left out.

I was devastated. Through the many disappointments I have had with selection over the years, I would have to say this one knocked me down the most. It just didn't make sense to me: if I couldn't keep my place after that, what more could I do?

Prior to the side being announced I was called by the chairman of selectors, Trevor Hohns. The reason he gave me was the old 'horses for courses', which I obviously disagreed with. I'd had a lot of success at the Gabba when playing for South Australia. We were playing England, a team I knew like the back of my hand, having played County cricket for years. If it was 'horses for courses' they were after, I felt like I was Kingston Town running around Moonee Valley.

Still, there isn't much you can do when the selectors make their call. You're out, simple as that, and all the well-wishers who ring to offer their condolences don't help ease the pain.

Ricky Ponting came back into the side and I went back to South Australia determined to prove to the selectors I was good enough to command a spot in the side. As it turned out I had a good start to the summer, and Ricky found runs hard to come by in that series. By the Fourth Test I found myself back in the side. I thought I should never have been left out in the first place, but when I was brought back in, I was suddenly under enormous pressure for the first time in my brief Test career.

Admittedly it was mostly pressure I was placing on myself, but after having been dropped, I now had two Tests to prove I was worthy of selection. As loose as I felt going into that Bangalore Test, I was equally as tight and tense heading into the Boxing Day match against England.

It's hard to explain why you get like that. It's something you have very little control over, especially when you are just starting out. I have heard top tennis players own up to getting nervous in the fifth set of big matches and golfers have admitted the same thing. I was definitely way too tense going into those two matches.

As a consequence I batted poorly. The highest score I made in four innings was 32, at the SCG, where I also got a duck. I just didn't give myself a chance. I was going way too hard at the ball, trying to score too quickly, too early, and basically trying to be a player I wasn't. Instead of batting the same way I had for ten years, the same way I had in those first two Tests on the subcontinent, I went about it a different way and paid the price. I found myself back out of the side and to be honest I deserved to be. I got out in ridiculous ways, to bowlers I would normally feast on. Basically, I let myself down.

As a batsman I never mind being dismissed by a good ball. Cricket is a game that will do that to you from time to time, no matter how good a player you are. But when you don't think clearly and give yourself the best chance to succeed, that's when you get really disappointed. I was pretty low at the end of that Ashes series. I had played poorly in my first home series and again was out of the Test team after starting so well earlier in the year.

If I was given an extended shot at the five-day game, I knew I was good enough to play well. But as I packed my bags for the World Cup in the West Indies I wasn't sure I was ever going to get that chance.

NINE
THE AUSTRALIAN TEAM: THE INNER SANCTUM

'What's it like being part of the Australian cricket team?' I wish I had a dollar for every time I've been asked that question. It's not easy to answer because there are so many different aspects to playing for Australia. Obviously the short answer is that it's awesome, but then you really need to break it down.

The first thing you notice when you start playing for Australia is the obsession this country has with its cricket team. It seems everything you do is watched by everyone – and not just while you are playing. I'm talking about going to breakfast at hotels, getting on and off the bus, sitting in airport departure lounges and dining at restaurants. You just can't escape the ever-watching crowds and, early on, when you get your first taste of it, you don't *want* to escape it – it's sensational.

I remember one night when I was first part of the Australian Test team, back in 1990, Merv Hughes and I decided to go out and take a look at the Sydney nightlife. We were in a taxi and the driver dropped us out the front of the biggest nightclub in the biggest city in Australia. This place was jumping. There was a queue a mile long, red carpet, bouncers, the lot.

I got out of the taxi and joined the queue. Merv finished

paying the driver and then looked up to see me standing on the end of this massive line-up.

He said, 'What the hell do you think you're doing?'

'Standing in the line,' I said.

'Pig's arse,' said the big fella, and started walking to the front door with me, a naive twenty-year-old from Adelaide, in tow.

Through we went, with all these people in the line getting angry with us for pushing in – and fair enough, too. Once inside, the crowd parted as we made our way up to the bar, where we weren't expected to pay for a drink for the next four hours. It was all on the house – they were just excited to have us socialising at their club.

The manager came down asking us if everything was okay. The place was teeming with beautiful people, we weren't paying a cent and everyone wanted to talk to us – how could that not be okay as a young fellow? I'd never experienced anything like that before.

I've heard other players say playing with the Aussies is like being in a cocoon, and in a funny way they are right. You do live in a kind of bubble and you really need to be on your game as a person to not get consumed by it.

One of the great things about the Australian teams I have played with is that no-one is allowed to get carried away with the hype. It just isn't tolerated. Allan Border, the Australian skipper when I was first involved, was very big on that. You showed the game, the team and the people around the team respect at all times. It wasn't your God-given right as a Test player to demand something for nothing and A.B. made sure you understood that right from the start. The honeymoon only lasts as long as you're a part of the team and Allan Border, along with other senior players like David Boon and Geoff Marsh, was always quick to point out that all the attention dried up pretty quickly if you stopped making runs.

The exposure to famous people is another thing that still amazes me. For a guy who left school at seventeen and worked in a Holden factory, to be talking one-on-one to an Oscar-winning actor such as Russell Crowe is bizarre. Funny thing is, I found Russell was just like us guys. He's easygoing, down to earth and loves his cricket. He also loves a beer and a joke, and is seemingly totally unaffected by his fame.

Current and former prime ministers come into the dressing rooms from time to time, and we often see the boys from INXS and Powderfinger around the place; they love their cricket as much as we all love their music.

You might run into television stars, especially in cities such as Melbourne and Sydney, although it helps if you hang around with Shane Warne, who knows them all. Warnie is our most famous player and all the celebrities gravitate towards him.

It constantly amazes me that so many people love the game of cricket and want to get close to the Australian team. I love meeting people from all walks of life; I myself was an avid cricket fan as a youngster and in many ways still am. I still love to meet the players I admire from today or the past.

The cricket fans in Australia are sensational and you are pretty much always happy to sign an autograph and have a chat. The only time this can become a problem is on game day, especially when you are playing Tests and one-day internationals in Australia. Then the team is obviously much more in demand.

There are times when the crowds are so intense it's all you can do to get from the change-rooms to the nets to practise.

The big one-day matches are the worst for this. You might get 80,000 at the MCG for a day–night game and it can become almost impossible for players to move around.

I like to sign everything; I don't worry about things like whether the person is going to sell it on the Internet; for every one of them there are 1000 genuine lovers of the game who want something signed as a memento of their day watching the Australian team. So, where I can, I sign until there are no autograph hunters left. But you just can't do that on game day – it's impossible.

You are basically at work and can't afford to let yourself get distracted, not by kids wanting things signed, not by mates wanting to say hello, not by tourists wanting a photo. You've got an hour and a half to prepare for an international match and you need every second of that time. People often find that hard to understand. I can't remember how many times I have heard people get upset when you decline a signature request on the day of a match. 'It would only take a second,' they say.

That might be true, but how do you turn the next kid down if you have just stopped a second earlier? You stop once and it's like a feeding frenzy, and as soon as you get stuck in the middle of that you lose valuable time from of your preparation. It's also a case of just trying to get through the mass of people. Cricket is a unique game like this. In football you come from the changerooms and through a tunnel onto the ground. In golf you have stewards keeping the fans away, but at cricket grounds you have to make your way from the nets to the dressing room, and to do that you have to walk, unprotected, through the crowd.

Then there is the problem of actually getting out on to the ground. At my home ground in Adelaide the first 40 metres of your journey out to bat are basically through the crowd. You've got to jostle past members who are taking the fall of a wicket as an opportunity to have a toilet break, there are people carrying drink trays, hot dogs and chips, trying to keep their kids under control – and there you are attempting to get out to the centre to face Shoaib Akhtar.

So game day can be a bit hectic. That said though, there are plenty of people there to make your life easier. Coaches, assistant coaches, physiotherapists, masseurs, trainers, net bowlers, ball boys ... you name it, they are there, and they are all there for one reason: to make it easier for you to play well.

As a club player you have to twist your mate's arm to come and give you some throw-downs. As a first-class cricketer you can have a hit before the day's play, but if you want one once the day is underway you need to beg, borrow and steal. But if you are playing for Australia, there are usually four or five young hopefuls just waiting to bowl to a Test player. You can bat in the nets for hours on end if you want to. They have bowling machines; the balls are either brand new or as good as; the nets are top quality and they are never being used by anyone else.

One thing cricket fans around the world seem intrigued with is what it's like inside the Australian dressing room on game day.

The Australian dressing room is unlike any other sporting change-room I have come across; it is a real 'inner sanctum'. People who don't belong there are not allowed in. You get the players, coaches, medical staff, trainers and the odd room attendant and that's basically it. There is always someone on the door to make sure you have clearance before you're able to step inside, and anyone who wants to invite a guest has to get the captain's clearance first. That way it is kept just for the players and I will tell you why this is so important.

With the media scrutiny so great on the Australian team in modern times, the players are rarely able to let their hair down. You can't use the language you want, you can't wear whatever you like, you can't act like an idiot, carry on like a total fool or have a sleep during the middle of the day.

Every movement you make during a game, and these days even away from the ground, can be caught by someone holding a camera. Players at this level have to expect that, so the dressing room takes on enormous importance. Once you are in there, your time is yours and you can do whatever and be whoever you like. That's why there is such fascination about what goes on in there; outside the players' homes, it is really the only place the public aren't allowed.

On game day there is always plenty of noise, the stereo is always pumping and the mood is very 'up', especially on day one of a Test match. It doesn't matter whether it's the First Test of a series or if we are 3–1 up, on the first day of a Test the players are very toey and that always leads to plenty of noise.

The worst people for this are the bowlers: Glenn McGrath, Jason Gillespie, Brett Lee, Andy Bichel, Stuart MacGill. They all make way too much noise in the change-room before play, especially when they find out they don't have to bowl. In fact, they make way too much noise all day. I don't know whether it's because they are bored or nervous, but unless they are next in to bat you simply cannot shut them up. There's that old saying, 'Empty vessels make the most noise'. Batsmen always say you have to be stupid to be a bowler so perhaps that's why they find it impossible to be quiet? But more about them in a moment.

The batsmen have a very different way of getting ready on the first day of a Test match. For them, it's 'game on', it's business, and every player I have ever played with at that level has a different way of preparing.

As a batsman you have a little over thirty minutes to get yourself mentally ready to go, because the toss happens about 10.20 on the first morning. The two openers I have played most with, Justin Langer and Matthew Hayden, could not be more different in the half-hour before the first ball is bowled.

Hayden is a strong man, both physically and mentally, and he likes to get himself almost into a trance-like state before the action starts. He takes himself right away from all the noise and the banter; he goes into another part of the dressing room, perhaps to the rub-down room or the viewing room where it is quiet, and he gets himself ready.

For 'Haydos', it's war. He is going out to battle and wants to really focus on what's about to occur. He's a gladiator in a real sense. I know that may sound strange but that's what he's like. It's almost as if he is putting on the armour and he's about to explode into the arena to tame the lions and tigers and whatever else the opposition can throw at him.

No-one speaks to Matt before play starts. Everyone leaves him alone and as he walks through the rooms to go onto the ground he says the same words every time: 'Good luck boys'.

Langer is the complete opposite. He loves loud music, jumping around; he loves the vibe being up and he loves being happy. That's what he needs to go out and play good cricket. The more up-tempo the dressing room, the better. It's like a football mentality. His father and brothers were all footballers and it shows in his body language before the game.

He always has the earphones in and turns the sound up loud. It's like someone has plugged him into a light socket. Basically, what you see as he walks on to the ground is what he has been like for the previous fifteen minutes. He feeds off the positive vibe that always exists in the Australian rooms. Justin being pumped fires us up and the more we get pumped watching how 'up' he is, the more pumped he gets.

Ricky Ponting has no set routine other than his own superstitions. He never seems to be overly hyped and he never seems to be very nervous or edgy. This is one of the reasons why he is such a good leader. You wouldn't know what 'Punter' is thinking about the task ahead, because he is always the same – steady, focused and positive, but not insular to the point where no-one feels comfortable approaching him, and that's important when you are the captain as well as one of the team's best players.

There is no point Ricky getting too fired up anyway, because the openers regularly put on 150, which means he doesn't bat until after drinks in the second session.

I am pretty similar to Ricky. I have never seen the point of getting too carried away before going out to bat. I will be ready when it comes my turn and have always found the more relaxed I am, the better I play. Also, the older I get, the calmer I am. Results are not so important, the process I work by is. I'm there to play the best I can to help the team win the game.

I don't believe it helps the players around you, especially the younger ones, if you are too intense prior to going out to bat. The rookies tend to absorb the body language and attitudes of the senior players, so I always try to be as happy and easygoing as possible, which enables them to enjoy their time in the dressing room. The happier a team is, the better it will play – that has always been my experience, no matter which sport or level of the sport.

Damien Martyn is a little more particular about the way he gets ready. He's got those Hollywood looks and he takes a little more time over his appearance than I do. His gear has to be just right and he is not happy until every 'i' is dotted and every 't' crossed. That's the way he is and everyone in the team respects it.

Basically, no-one cares what it takes as long as you are ready to go when the wicket falls and you are next in. And when you are the next in to bat your wish is the team's command. If you want a drink, someone will get one for you. If you want to sit in a certain spot, it's yours. If you want a bit of toast buttered with Vegemite on the half-hour, you'll get it as long as you are the next player in to bat.

As soon as you are out it's all bets off and you get it yourself. The next batsman in is the most important figure in the Australian team's rooms.

The Waugh boys were as different as Matty Hayden and Justin Langer.

Mark Waugh was always a very funny man in the rooms; very dry, and master of the one-liners. You could never tell that 'Junior' was the next man in because his demeanour never changed. He just sat there, read the paper and talked to anyone who was prepared to listen. At times Mark Waugh would start reading just to stop himself from dozing off to sleep. I am serious. It was probably a mixture of nerves and being the most relaxed man on the planet but he would dead-set nearly nod off waiting to bat.

Steve, on the other hand, was much more focused. He would chew through packet after packet of chewing gum and watch intently. His face had the 'gunfighter' stare that was so famous at the crease. He might pick up a paper or read a book, but only for five minutes to change the routine a little. He wasn't really taking in what he was reading, he just needed to do something different.

Some players don't like to watch what's going on out in the middle too much. They think they'll see it all for themselves when they get out there. Stephen wasn't like that; he watched like a hawk.

Adam Gilchrist is quite quiet when he's waiting to go out, which is a little strange for a guy who is normally so happy-go-lucky. He tends to sit in his own area and watch and take it all in without saying anything or dominating the room. He is about to dominate the bowling and it's like he knows it and is saving himself to do exactly that. Unlike a lot of the other batsmen in the Aussie side whose style on the ground mirrors their behaviour in the rooms, the Adam Gilchrist waiting to bat is nothing like the man who plasters the opposition to all parts of the ground.

Shane Warne is often called 'Hollywood' because he regularly has mail up to knee-height in the rooms and has to plough through it. Managers and media people are always knocking on the door wanting a piece of him and he spends a lot of time on the phone, diary out, organising business, massages, physio, all the things that make him play to the standard we all know and love. It's not as free and easygoing for Warnie as it is for the rest of us. It may sound like he gets special treatment, but he doesn't. He is still very much a team man and a great lover of his team-mates, but it's a little strange in 'Shane's World' and we all respect that.

The fast bowlers follow and they are grouped together because they are all so similar. When they are preparing to bowl they are pumping themselves right up. They will get ready to bowl in partnerships, especially Jason Gillespie and Glenn McGrath, who have had such an amazing amount of success bowling in tandem.

Brett Lee is a great addition to any dressing room. He loves being in there and he just wants everyone to succeed, whether it's a batsman or a bloke who's vying for the same spot as him. He is a genuine team man, which I really love about him. He wants the ball after 'Dizzy' and 'Pidge' have finished with it and he wants to bowl fast.

Glenn McGrath is a pest and I mean that in the nicest possible way. You will be sitting there minding your own business and suddenly a sugar sachet will be emptied in your hair or a feather will be tickling you behind the ear and you think it's a fly. He basically gets bored quickly and takes it out on everyone else. It must be a fast bowler thing because Merv Hughes used to do exactly the same thing.

Jason Gillespie gets plenty of stick in the rooms and most of it surrounds the length of his nose. When he first started playing he just sat there and didn't say boo but now he gives as good as he gets, and so he should as a senior and much-loved player in the side. For years 'Dizzy' has been desperate to have his batting taken seriously and will tell everyone who's prepared to hear him out that he has a Test century in him.

The bowler's lot has changed drastically in recent times. When I started, if the team was batting first the bowlers could do pretty much what they liked until they were unlucky enough to have to pull on the pads.

Now they are in the hands of Errol Alcott and Jock Campbell, the fitness advisers attached to the team. If the openers are putting on a big stand, the fast bowlers may be taken to the gym to do some aerobic fitness work. They could do a weights session and if there is a pool available they could be sent there to do some laps. As the innings winds down they will be thoroughly stretched and warmed up so they are 100 per cent ready to go when the last wicket falls.

The same goes for the batsmen. If you have been dismissed for not many and haven't spent much time in the middle, one of the fitness guys will grab you and out you go to do a full-on session of whatever takes their fancy. It's a great incentive to stay out in the middle, I assure you.

So cricket change-rooms have changed a lot in recent times. Gone are the days when players just lounged around and watched their mates out in the middle. Sure, there is still some of that going on, but the 'down' time is used much more than it ever was and even though the players complain, it does make a lot of sense.

A Test match lasts five days and if the team bats once and you don't get many, that's a lot of time spent sitting around and nothing will make you unfit more quickly than lounging around watching someone else doing what you should be doing yourself.

The other area where cricket dressing rooms have definitely

changed is after stumps. Gone are the times when you would start enjoying your first beer five minutes after the last ball was bowled. Now there are ice baths, warm-down spa sessions, all stuff I have to say I don't enjoy because the ice baths are too bloody cold!

But the good thing about the way John Buchanan and Ricky Ponting (and Steve Waugh before him) run the Australian team is that after you have finished all that is required of you by the fitness and medical team, you can do whatever you want. There is no curfew – you are never told you can't go to this place or mix with those people. Your time is your own and you can do with it what you like, as long as you are on deck at the required time the next day and in a fit state to do the job required of you.

The last thing I will mention about the 'inner sanctum' is the enormous pressure placed on the Australian captain. It's something most observers find hard to comprehend. As a player you don't get to see a lot of the skipper after hours, especially when the Test matches are played in Australia, because he carries an enormous load and is asked to do so much more than everyone else.

He handles most of the media for a start. Every so often a player who has played really well will relieve him of that responsibility, but normally it's the captain who fronts the press. If a board member or selector comes into the rooms, nine times out of ten they need to speak to the skipper. Any issues with people like match referees or umpires will go through the captain. Planning for training sessions, travel schedules, even the location of hotels, will need to be cleared by the man in charge. While I can just get my own act together and wander back to the hotel whenever I please, Ricky generally has his agenda set for him and even though he tries to stay with us as much as possible, it is often very difficult. In fact, you need to remember at times to make sure he is invited with the rest of the players to a restaurant or bar, because often he gets so inundated he misses the fun everyone else is having.

So that's a look in the Australian dressing room. It's a great place to spend some time and players who've been lucky enough to make it in never want to leave.

TEN
WORLD
CUP
WONDER

While I spent many years striving to get into the Australian Test team, I'd been regularly selected to play in the one-day side. For a while I was considered a 'one-day specialist' who might never play Test cricket. I have always loved the shortened version of the game. The holy grail of one-day cricket is the World Cup, when every cricket-playing nation of note in the world descends on one region every four years for the right to say they are the best one-day team in the game.

World Cup cricket has given me some of the most special moments in my career. Australia has won three World Cups and I was in the fortunate position of hitting the winning runs in 1999 and then taking the winning catch in 2003.

As a player you don't think about hitting the winning runs. It really isn't something you focus on too much – you just want to win the game and whoever hits the runs gets you to that win. That said, if you are at the crease when the opportunity arises, you want to do it properly and I thank Saqlain Mushtaq for the half-tracker in 1999 because it looks so much better bringing up the win with a boundary than with a scrambled single. I always remember David Boon winning Australia back the Ashes in 1989 with a sweep shot for four. It is a piece of vision that has been played over and over again and so it should: it's part of Australian sporting history.

The two World Cup campaigns I have been a part of involved two totally different sides and two vastly different tournaments, but thankfully the result on both occasions was the same – the Australian captain holding aloft the trophy.

The Australian team that travelled to England for the 1999 tournament was nowhere near the powerhouse that boarded the plane for South Africa four years later. We were the tournament favourites in 1999, but in my opinion were not as good a side as we were four years later. Steve Waugh was the captain, and his position in the side had started to be questioned by cricket observers. His form in the one-day international series in Australia the previous summer had been indifferent and, like Mark Taylor before him, some were starting to say that his right to automatic selection in both teams was in doubt.

Shane Warne had been playing with serious injury and was finding it difficult to carry the considerable load he had previously shouldered with ease. And Jason Gillespie wasn't available at all through injury. Unlike in 2003, when we had the best one-day team in the game by a mile and everyone was fit and raring to go, this was an Australian side that, while very strong, had its share of problems.

In England we got off to an ordinary start. After beating Scotland we struggled to get some momentum going, dropping games to New Zealand and Pakistan. In the end we were probably fortunate to make it into the second round.

In my opinion a couple of things during that time conspired to turn the trip around – they were completely different, yet in a funny way the same.

The first one was that the drinking ban that had been placed on the team by the coach, Geoff Marsh, and Steve Waugh was abolished after about a month. I have never been a believer in telling grown men what they can and can't do. Having a social drink as a cricketer has been an important part of the mental relaxation required to play the game. While that may be changing in some circles, in 1999 it was still very much the done thing. I am not talking about staying out the night before a match until closing time and drinking so much that you can't function properly the next day. Those days are long gone at any decent level of cricket and so they should be.

But you can't tell a group of Australian cricketers who are together on the road for a long time that they aren't allowed to have a drink together. That is only ever going to lead to a bunch of unhappy blokes.

It might sound strange to someone outside the sport, especially people like elite track athletes who never touch alcohol as part of their rigorous training and practice routines. But when you are a member of a team that is on the road for months on end, the social side of the equation is very important.

Eventually a group of senior players went to Steve and Geoff and quietly pointed out that this drinking ban wasn't working. Thankfully, they decided to drop it and as soon as the ban was lifted the team improved. The whole feeling around the group was much better, spirits were lifting and it showed in the middle.

The other thing we did after that first month was pick a more balanced team, and that coincided with the inclusion of Tom Moody. The big fellow from the west was originally famous as a big-hitting batsman. He had actually been picked to play Test cricket as a batsman and had made two centuries. But the difference he made to our team back in 1999 was as a bowler. We had McGrath, Reiffel, Fleming and Warne all playing, but the fifth bowler was proving to be a real problem.

Given that Adam Gilchrist was opening, if we went in with five specialist bowlers it left the middle order very light on and yet if we picked an extra batsman, that fifth bowling spot became very vulnerable. As soon as Moody came in, it was problem solved. He bowled his ten overs very economically on almost every occasion and he was the perfect batsman to come in at number seven.

I say these two problems were strangely linked because no player on that 1999 tour was keener for the alcohol ban to be lifted than big Tom. He is passionate about enjoying his cricket after hours and the inability to enjoy a beer at the bar was killing him.

What also helped to turn things around was some of the best one-day batting I have ever seen from our captain, Steve Waugh, dispelling all speculation about his right to be in the team. As I mentioned, he'd been out of sorts in the one-day arena. He really hadn't taken any form at all into the tournament and his first month of batting gave no indication of was to come.

There had been much said, even before we landed in England in 1999, about the rivalry between South Africa and Australia. There is no doubt Australia has had the wood over the South Africans in both forms of the game since they came back to world cricket in the early 1990s. And there is nothing that annoys a South African more than having to admit that Australians are better than them at anything.

Coming into 1999 I got the feeling that the South Africans, under Hansie Cronje, thought they had their best chance of knocking us off. They had a very talented team – Jacques Kallis, Jonty Rhodes, Hansie himself, Lance Klusener, a very strong bowling attack led by Allan Donald and a top wicket-keeper–batsman in Mark Boucher.

So when we met them in the Super Sixes, there was much discussion about the mental edge we were supposed to have over our friends from across the Indian Ocean.

The South African camp claimed that we had branded them 'chokers', a serious allegation in sporting circles. Stephen said that he had never used that word; all he had said was that our team handled pressure better than they did.

This was the atmosphere coming into the match that ultimately, I think, won us the World Cup. We carried no points into the Super Sixes, having dropped three games in the qualifying round. We couldn't afford to lose a match during the second round or we would be out of the tournament. In other words, we were under pressure.

The South Africans, on the other hand, were in much better form. They were in the other group and arguably they had played better than anyone else in the first half of the World Cup. Unlike us, they could drop a game in the second round and still advance to the semi-finals.

So when we met in that Super Sixes match at Headingley there was plenty more than just bragging rights on the line.

For the second stage of the tournament Stephen had really started to embrace the mantra of 'backing yourself'. He had a sign placed on the team bus and he repeated it over and over to every player in the team: 'If you think you can do it, back yourself and go for it'. Basically, he was saying 'Never die wondering, have a crack and if you fail, at least you gave it your best shot'. The obvious message was that you are far more likely to succeed if you back yourself than if you allow doubt to creep in. At the team meeting the night before, he reiterated this line of thinking.

The other interesting thing that was discussed at that meeting was the unique catching style of one of the South African players, Herschelle Gibbs. Shane Warne said he had observed Gibbs throwing the ball up almost before he had it in his hands. Warnie even suggested that anyone caught by Gibbs the next day should stand their ground and wonder if he had the ball in his hands long enough to claim the catch. We all dismissed this as left-field rubbish and a few of us actually told Warnie as much, but it was amazing how relevant that comment was the next day. They were prophetic words indeed.

I wasn't in the side for the Headingley match as I'd broken my finger a week earlier against Zimbabwe. The future of the side was riding on one match and I was not able to do a thing about it.

We got to the ground and there was an eerie feeling right from the start; it was as if the ground knew that something special was about to happen. The place was calm and quiet. We won the toss and elected to bowl because we thought the pitch at Leeds traditionally did a bit and we preferred to know how many we needed batting second.

It was a good plan on paper but the South Africans absolutely belted hell out of us, making seven for 271 on a pitch that should never have coughed up that many. I believe that if we had lost that match, Stephen would have been stripped of the captaincy and some senior players in the one-day side would have gone down with him. That fact alone made the run chase even more spectacular. The dressing rooms at Headingley during that lunchbreak were deadly quiet. Everyone was aware of what the rest of the day meant.

As we started our chase it didn't look like we were going to make it to 170, let alone top 271. Mark Waugh was run out for five, Adam Gilchrist was also dismissed for five and Damien Martyn went for 11. At three for 48 in the twelfth over we were in real strife and it took a fine hand of 69 from Ricky Ponting to start turning things our way. As he always does, he attacked the quick bowlers, square-cutting and pulling. Even though we were looking down the barrel he gave the dressing room some sort of confidence that all wasn't lost.

Ricky and Stephen put on 126 for the fourth wicket and once Ponting departed, Michael Bevan joined the captain. The run rate was starting to climb – I think we needed more than seven an over from about the halfway mark – and Stephen decided that the moment had come. It was sink or swim, Sydney or the bush, however you want to put it.

He was on 56 when he tried to flick the ball through the on-side. The bat sort of turned in his hands and the ball ballooned to Gibbs, fielding at his customary mid-wicket position. Just as Warnie had predicted the night before, Herschelle tried to take the ball and throw it skywards in the same motion. To the horror and dismay of every South African on the planet, he dropped the ball. It was an absolute sitter and one of their best fielders had turfed it.

What followed has gone down in Australian sporting folk-lore and in true Aussie fashion we haven't let the truth get in the way of a good story.

Prior to the catch being dropped, Gibbs had started chirping away at Steve, saying things like, 'Let's see how the superstar can handle the pressure now, boys' and 'Seven an over, who can handle this sort of pressure?'. He was, of course, harking back to the comments Steve had made in the press conference.

So when Gibbs dropped the catch, Stephen pinned his ears back and gave him both barrels. If you hear it told at your local pub, it generally goes along the lines of Stephen turning to Gibbs and saying, 'Well done, mate, you've just dropped the World Cup'. Which would have been an all-time line given that we went on to win the trophy! But that is not what Stephen said. As much as we would all love it to be true, he said it wasn't.

What he said to Gibbs went along the lines of: 'That's what I mean about pressure, we can take it and you can't – you've just cost your team the match'.

Given that we were four down and needed more than seven an over, it was still an enormously ballsy thing to say, but from that moment Stephen was like a man possessed. He played some of the most amazing shots I have seen, slog sweeping quick bowlers over mid-wicket for six, flat-batting balls over wide mid-off, even pull and hook shots that he rarely played. It was like watching him ten years earlier. He decided to risk the lot and go crazy, and it was extraordinary to watch.

In the dressing rooms we all sensed that the wheel was start-ing to turn our way; the little things in a game of cricket that can go either way were favouring us. Michael Bevan supported Stephen beautifully and they put together a stand of 73. But when Bevan went for 27 we still needed more than a run a ball with Tom Moody our last recognised batsman.

Stephen took it upon himself to get us over the line that day and in the process played one of the greatest one-day innings in the history of the game. I have seen some brilliant one-day innings played all around the world, but consider the circumstances of this one. He carried the expectations of his country, his captaincy and his position in the team were both on the line, and there was the simmering feud with the opposition.

When Steve scored the winning runs in the last over the dressing rooms erupted. You had to see it to believe it. We had dodged a massive bullet on the back of his brilliant 120 not out off only 110 balls and we were still alive in the competition.

Players were jumping around and hugging each other – it was pure pandemonium. Stephen was as excited as I had ever seen him and why *wouldn't* he be? So much pressure had been placed on him and suddenly he had made runs, the best kind of runs (to borrow a phrase from Dennis Cometti) and we were through to the semis. The whole team had come full circle, from a team that was uptight and playing badly to a team that was relaxed and backing itself to attack and win.

The party after the win at Headingley was as big as any I had experienced as a member of an Aussie team. It went through into the next morning for some of us. We didn't have to play again for eight days and really let loose. Looking back, I think the reason behind that was relief. We had made it to the semi-finals of the World Cup and that meant we couldn't be considered failures. The pressure was off.

In the days following the match we all started to think we would go on to make the final. To beat South Africa, a very good side, in a match we had no right to win made us believe we were destined to go to the top. That sounds like a big statement and it was almost proved wrong a week later when we turned around and played the same team in a semi-final that was filled with just as much drama, and in a way is probably more famous.

We had trained the house down in Birmingham in the lead-up to the semi-final against South Africa. People watching us training couldn't believe the difference from the Australian team that had dragged its butt through the first half of the tournament. We were upbeat, the jokes were flying again, and the players were looking forward to playing the match rather than dreading another poor performance. Momentum is a huge thing in sport and we certainly had it.

It was more a case of '*momentum, schmomentum*' once the semi-final started, however. We batted first and again were in all sorts of trouble from the start. We lost early wickets and really, aside from Steve Waugh (56) and Michael Bevan (65), we didn't bat very well at all. The wicket was doing a little bit, but it was certainly not dangerous or overly difficult to score on, so when we finished with 213 on the board many thought we were in real strife.

I wasn't panicking, because I always reckon when you ask the side batting second to score more than four an over in a final you are still in the game. That may sound like optimistic thinking, and plenty of that goes on in a cricketer's head, but I honestly believed if we bowled and fielded well we could still place enormous pressure on the South Africans.

Again we struggled early, this time with the ball, and the South Africans had almost 50 on the board quite quickly without losing any wickets.

Twice in as many games we had dug ourselves into a hole and twice it took a champion to get us over the line. In Leeds it was Stephen; in Birmingham it was Shane Warne.

Warnie hadn't had a great time with the ball in the early parts of the tour; he had been bowling tightly but not getting the wickets normally expected from him. As with Steve, it had been playing on his mind. So when he took the ball in the semi-final with the opposition none down and needing about 160, he was probably thinking like the rest of us – there was never going to be a better time for some Warne magic.

Not many know that during the break between the matches against South Africa, Steve Waugh had taken Shane for a walk in Hyde Park, and they'd had an old-fashioned heart-to-heart. Shane's shoulder had been giving him real trouble, he had been copping it from the press about his weight, and with the wickets not going his way there was talk he might be heading out of the one-day arena. But Steve settled him down during the walk, by telling him to let the future look after itself. He told him to relax and let everything go, to give the ball a massive rip and see how the cards fell.

And didn't he turn it on?

Warnie is a big-game performer – he has proved that time and again. And this day he bowled beautifully. The fizz was back on the ball, the drift was there from the start and the batsmen were immediately under the sort of pressure you don't need when you are trying to win a final.

Gibbs, Kirsten and Cronje were all gone, courtesy of the

master, and the game was turned on its ear. South Africa went from a position of strength to being vulnerable very quickly and we certainly picked up on that out on the field.

We knew they didn't like pressure, and we already had the upper hand from the match at Headingley. The vibe on the ground changed completely on the back of one spell of bowling.

That said, the game wasn't safe; far from it. Kallis and Rhodes did a great job of keeping them on track with a stand of 84, but the problem for the South Africans was that they lost wickets at exactly the wrong time; just when they looked like getting on top, a wicket would fall and the tension would mount again.

We got the asking rate to around six an over, which was a great job considering we were defending 213.

But all that was to change when Lance Klusener decided to go bananas. Swinging hard and invariably connecting, he had been awesome throughout the tournament and he threatened to rip this game apart with some of the cleanest hitting you ever saw.

This time *we* were feeling the pressure; we dropped Klusener, misfields started creeping in, I missed a run-out that I should have taken and as a side we were right in the crosshairs.

It all came down to the last over. South Africa needed nine runs to win, we needed one wicket and Damien Fleming was bowling to Klusener.

Klusener hit the first two balls of the over for four. Well, that's not quite right – he absolutely belted them for four. If the fence hadn't been there the ball would have rolled into the next county.

Now we were really down and out ... four balls to defend

one run with their strike batsman facing and seeing them awfully well.

Klusener hit the third ball straight to me. I picked it up and saw Donald had taken off for the run. If I hit the stumps now it was game over and we were through to the final.

I missed.

I thought we were cooked. I thought it had been our last roll of the dice and I felt terrible.

The next delivery was a dot ball, so we were down to two balls to go and one run required.

What followed was one of the most astounding things I have seen on a cricket field. Klusener bottom-edged an attempted slog back down the ground and Mark Waugh came across from mid-off and attempted to run him out with a backhand flick. That's right – a backhand flick in the last over of a final, if you don't mind. He was the only man on the planet cool enough to even attempt such a thing.

But Donald, who had almost been run out two balls earlier, wasn't backing up this time. If he had, South Africa would have won the game. He didn't, and a cool-thinking Fleming relayed the ball along the ground to Adam Gilchrist. Donald wasn't in the picture.

Amazingly, we had tied the game with 213 runs each, but, because we'd beaten them in the Super Six stage, we knew straightaway we had won a place in the final. We had won the match in the most amazing circumstances and went nuts.

A photographer captured the moment perfectly, all eleven of us charging in from all directions, all in the photo. We were floating, the excitement of winning pumping through our veins. Just quietly, I was more than relieved after missing that run-out just moments before.

Unlike the previous match, the dressing rooms at Edgbaston were relatively quiet. I think everyone was mentally drained and those last thirty minutes had taken their toll. I have read about people who fought at war and then completely collapsed once the battle was over. This wasn't hand-to-hand combat or life and death, but we were utterly exhausted. It really touched nerve ends.

We were in the final, but the stupid thing was we still hadn't played the perfect game. We had batted well in the Headingley match and bowled and fielded well in the semi, but we still hadn't pieced it all together.

I must admit to feeling sorry for the South African players. They carried an enormous amount of expectation and pressure on their shoulders and this was meant to be their time to shine. They had lost two games in a row to us when they really should have won both. Hansie Cronje was furious in the rooms next door to ours; things were being thrown around and you could hear the swearing even from where we sat. I wouldn't have liked to be in there.

They had played much better than us throughout the tournament and had every right to expect a berth in the big game. Cronje actually came into our rooms after the game to congratulate Stephen along with everyone else and I admired him for that. He could easily have packed his stuff up and got out of there as quickly as possible, but he showed great courage coming into our rooms, as did all his team-mates. Blokes like Allan Donald were hurting but they all fronted up and they won a lot of respect from us by doing so.

The World Cup final was to be played against Pakistan at Lord's in three days' time, so there was no time for partying. The schedule was tight and we needed to get our act together for the decider.

All I remember about the morning of the final was being very nervous. As a rule I don't get nervous; I have always just played the game and had the required amount of confidence in my ability. But I remember being very tight this morning. We were in a final, at the home of cricket, in front of a packed house which included loyal Aussie fans a long way from home. And many back in Australia would be watching from their living rooms.

Lord's is a funny place. It's amazing looking, beautiful in the same way Adelaide Oval is beautiful, but they have strange rules over there. Women aren't allowed to sit in certain places, and, as a player, you are not allowed onto the ground unless you have your playing gear on. Unless you are officiating in the game, you are not allowed onto the playing surface, no matter who you are. I was lucky; I had been there before with Yorkshire so I wasn't thrown by all the procedure and pomp, and it was the same for most of our players. But when you go there for the first time it is a real spin-out.

In that match, we finally played the perfect game that we'd been looking for throughout the whole tournament. And it was all the more sweet that we won so convincingly. We were full of confidence, having faith in Steve's philosophy and truly believing we would be the winners.

We rolled Pakistan for 132 in thirty-nine overs and got the runs only two wickets down. When I was on strike and hit the winning runs with a boundary, the joy was beyond belief. I was the first Australian ever to do that, I found out later.

As Mark Waugh and I ran off the field we were swamped by people wanting to pat us on the back. It was magnificent to see the happiness on our fans' faces. By the time we reached the dressing room, faxes and phone calls of congratulations were already pouring in. It was the perfect ending to the campaign.

Seeing Stephen and Shane hold up the World Cup after all we had been through in the previous two months was brilliant. We had fought back from the brink of being group losers to become world champions. It had been an emotional rollercoaster, finally ending on an amazing high.

The celebrations at Lord's were long, with the singing of the team song led by Ricky Ponting up on big Tom Moody's shoulders at about 10.30 p.m. By this time we had been drinking for several hours, so you can imagine our singing was loud, if not exactly in tune. One thing we Australians know how to do is celebrate. Our team sponsor, Emirates Airlines, threw an enormous party that night at the hotel. It seemed as if they had invited every Australian in London, including many famous Aussie faces, and it lasted into the wee hours of the morning.

When we flew home to Australia, we were amazed by the reception from cricket fans. We flew in at night, yet the airport was packed with people congratulating us on our win. The Australian Cricket Board had flown all our families in to meet us, which was fantastic. Over the next few days we were honoured with tickertape parades in Melbourne and Sydney. All those people, crowding the streets and throwing streamers as we drove past – it was a scene you only ever expect to see on TV.

As a kid playing cricket in the backyard, I never dreamed I'd one day be a part of something like that. Back in Adelaide I was driven around the oval, World Cup in hand, at a footy match involving my beloved Adelaide Crows. I was so proud to be able to bring the cup home to show South Australians.

ELEVEN
THOSE TWO WORDS

I don't look back on things I have done in my cricketing career and worry too much about whether they make me feel proud, happy, ashamed, or anything else. It's not in my nature to do that. I tend to just front up and get on with it. I enjoy playing cricket and obviously I enjoy it more when we succeed, but I am not one of those people who carry achievements around like a badge of honour.

At my home there is almost no memorabilia. You won't see pictures of me playing or any framed shirts or caps. Maybe one day, when it's all over, I might mount a few pieces that I can look back on and be proud of.

But when I do look back, which isn't often, the one thing that usually springs to mind is something I wish I hadn't done. It happened on 15 January 2003, when Australia was playing a one-day international against Sri Lanka at the Gabba in Brisbane.

I was in really good form at the time. I was coming off a good summer in all forms of the game, especially in one-day cricket. After a period in the wilderness following the 1999 World Cup I had re-established myself as a regular member of the Australian one-day team. We were getting towards the

The bat and the pads are bigger than me, and how about that hair?

Above: Christmas Day in Whyalla, 1975.

Above right: Me sitting on my old man's pride and joy: his BSA Bantam.

Right: Proud as punch in my under-13s SAPSARSA uniform.

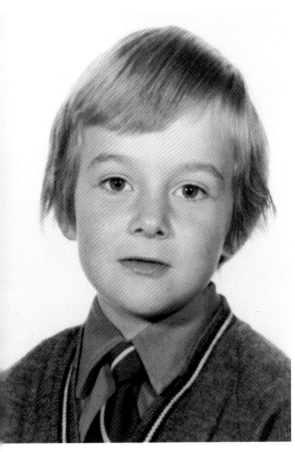

Early school years. Wish I'd tried as hard at school as I did at cricket.

Below: I'm next to the teacher (though I usually steered clear!).

MC, RITCHIE CRES
JUNIOR
PRIMARY SCHOOL
YEAR PREP 1 & 2
1975

Top: After hitting the winning runs, aged 11. Little did I know I'd do the same thing at Lord's 18 years later at the 1999 World Cup.

Bottom: My other passion – playing football, for Gawler Centrals. I'm the second from the right in the second row. My good mate Johnny Giannitto (second from the left in the front) was the one who give me the nickname 'Boof'.

Right: Playing with flair in the early days for South Australia. Check out the mullet!

Below: Enjoying a beer with a great mate and mentor, David Hookes, after a good day at the office, 1989.

A proud day: South Australia's Sheffield Shield win in 1995–96, at my favourite ground, the Adelaide Oval.

Getty Images/Graham Chadwick

Getty Images/Laurence Griffiths

Top: Mark Waugh and I running off the ground after winning the World Cup at Lord's in 1999.

Bottom: A proud moment for the boys: on the balcony at Lord's following our win.

Above: With my beautiful Andrea on our wedding day, 19 December 1999.

Left: Andrea with Amy and Ethan at my first home Test match at the Adelaide Oval, 23 November 2002.

Newspix/Mark Brake

Above: The tribe – Jake, Ethan, Tori, Amy and Andrea. I love them all so much.

Left: My number-one fan and source of constant support: Mum.

Top: Brothers-in-arms. My brother-in-law, Craig White, and I at the World Cup in South Africa, 2003.

Bottom: Time for a drink. Yorkshire celebrating their first County Championships win in 33 years, Scarborough, 2001. Celebrations went almost as long!

Left: An unbelievable moment. Scoring my first Test century in Trinidad, 2003. Notice how high I can get off the ground!

Below: Ricky Ponting, Adam Gilchrist, Matthew Hayden and I celebrating each scoring a century against the West Indies in Trinidad, 2003.

Newspix/Phil Hillyard

Newspix/Phil Hillyard

Getty Images/Hamish Blair

Top: Words of wisdom. Whenever I speak to groups of kids I encourage them to put more effort into their schoolwork than I ever did.

Bottom: Two of my great mates from the Australian side: 'Dizzy' and 'Punter'.

Left: One of the worst days of my life. Facing the media after the hearing, Adelaide, 2003.

Below: Andrea and I at the Allan Border Medal, cricket's version of the Brownlow, 2003.

Newspix/Jo-Anna Robinson

Newspix/Fiona Hamilton

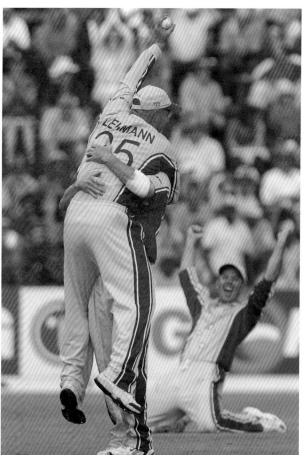

World Cup triumph: taking the catch to win the World Cup in Johannesburg, 2003. Damien Martyn almost broke his back lifting me up.

Getty Images/Stu Forster

Bowling for Australia in a one-day international in Zimbabwe, 2004. I seem to bowl more overs the older I get.

Newspix/Alexander Joe

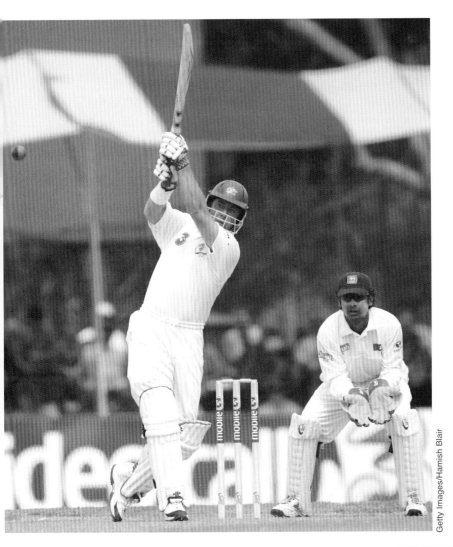

Getty Images/Hamish Blair

Above: On the attack aginst Sri Lanka in Darwin, 2004.

Right: Man of the Match (left) and Man of the Series (right). Sharing a moment with Shane Warne, Columbo, May 2004.

Getty Images/Sena Vidanagama

Galle, Sri Lanka, 2004. I firmly believe Hookesy was with me during the first part of this tour. When I brought up my century I looked up in thanks.

Blood, sweat and tears: a quiet moment during an emotional series in Sri Lanka. The heat was almost unbearable.

concluding stages of the VB Series and this match was against a Sri Lankan side that wasn't going to make the finals. England was the other team in the three-way competition.

I felt particularly good when I was batting, I was seeing the ball well, moving nicely and generally finding the middle of the bat. I'd reached about 40 and we were cruising to a comfortable victory, needing about four an over to win the match.

Even though we were doing it easy, I must admit I thought their attack was there for the taking and it was time for us to take a few risks, put the foot down and really finish them off. The fact that we weren't doing that was starting to frustrate me a little. While the result wasn't in doubt, the way we were playing wasn't to my liking.

I hit the ball to deep point and, coming back for the second run, took on the fielder when I shouldn't have. I wanted the strike back and momentarily forgot that I was a stumpy-legged waddler who wasn't going to win a sprint race anywhere.

Suddenly I was out, run out, and the frustration that had been building in me boiled over. I can't explain why I was so angry because we were in a very good position and, contrary to some people's idea of what occurred, no-one from the Sri Lankan team said a word after I was dismissed.

Truth is, I hadn't been happy for a while with parts of our one-day batting, and that day had been a great example of it.

Anger built up in me as I got closer and closer to the rooms and once in there I exploded, in the worst possible way. The two words I regrettably used were 'black c...s'. Contrary to the findings at a later hearing, I was well and truly inside our dressing room when I yelled out those words.

It is not something that I had said before and it certainly

isn't something I have said since, but on this occasion I did. Not only did I say it, but I said it way too loudly. Our team manager, Steve Bernard, who was in the change-rooms with me, left a few minutes later and was confronted by his counterpart Duleep Mendis, who had been in the Sri Lankan rooms down the corridor.

Mendis was pretty angry about what he had heard and rightly so. There is no excuse for those words ever being said, and he and the other people who were in the Sri Lankan rooms at the time had every right to be offended.

At this point Bernard came back into our rooms and told me that maybe I should apologise for my outburst. He explained the conversation he had just had with the opposition's management and made it very clear that they weren't impressed.

I then met Mendis and Sri Lankan coach Dav Whatmore, who I knew well from my days in Victoria, and who had also been in their rooms. I apologised instantly to them, saying I was very sorry they had to hear those words, that they were inexcusable and that they certainly weren't directed towards any individual. I acknowledged I was very wrong to have said them.

Dav said, 'No worries, don't worry about it, you have apologised straightaway' and he said he could tell my apology was genuine.

At that stage I thought that was the end of the matter. Nevertheless I also decided to draft a letter to the Sri Lankan camp, officially apologising for my inappropriate behaviour. I wrote the letter and when I finished it I walked into the Sri Lankan rooms and handed it to their captain, Sanath Jayasuriya. I apologised verbally to him and his team. I explained exactly what had happened, I owned up to what I had said and I wholeheartedly apologised for the hurt I had caused the people within earshot.

That the words were said in the heat of the moment and stemmed from frustration was absolutely no excuse. As a professional sportsman I should have been able to handle frustration and disappointment better and I was embarrassed and humiliated by what I had said.

The Sri Lankan players were sensational. They heard me out and then thanked me for having the courage to front them. I think they realised that what I said was out of character, at least I hope they did. Nothing they said or did after that meeting in their rooms gave me any indication that they felt the matter should go any further.

To this day I still do not know why I used those words. Colour doesn't come into thoughts I have of people; they are either good people or they are not. I honestly never consider whether they are black or white or any other colour. It is not an issue with me and perhaps that was where I let myself down.

But being called 'black' bothers coloured people a lot and that is something I didn't give enough credence to. 'Fat' doesn't bother me, but 'black' really bothers them.

After verbally apologising to the Sri Lankan group and handing them the letter of apology, I was called in to speak to the match referee, the former West Indian great Clive Lloyd. Duleep Mendis, Dav Whatmore and Steve Bernard joined me in the meeting with Lloyd.

Lloyd started by saying that the language I had used in the dressing rooms earlier that day could not be condoned. I explained to him that I had apologised instantly to the Sri

Lankan coach, then after the match to their whole touring party. I also mentioned the letter of apology.

I told Lloyd what I had told the Sri Lankan players, that I was very disappointed with what I had said, and I agreed with him that there was no way such language should be condoned. I also asked him what more he wanted me to do, because I was willing to do all I could to express my regret at the whole incident.

The Sri Lankan representatives at the meeting then supported what I said. They also stated that they didn't want to press any charges. As far as they were concerned the matter had been dealt with swiftly and appropriately.

Lloyd then wrapped it up by saying he was disappointed that it had been said in the first place, but he accepted that I had shown immediate and heartfelt remorse and he indicated that the matter was now resolved.

I was verbally reprimanded and told to make sure it didn't happen again. On that day, that was considered to be appropriate action from the match referee who was there acting on behalf on the International Cricket Committee (ICC). So on departure from that room I thought the matter would not go any further. I had been put on notice to make sure it never happened again, I had put myself on the same notice, and as we all walked out, the Sri Lankan representatives, Bernard and I were happy to put the whole thing behind us.

Little did I know that it was just the start. That night a Sri Lankan match reporter placed a story on the Baggy Green website describing the details of what had happened. He went to print with the exact words I had used and from there all hell broke loose. Something that to that point had been kept in house was now making headlines in newspapers around the world, along the lines of: 'Darren Lehmann racially slurs Sri Lankans'.

I first heard about it on the way from the hotel to Brisbane airport. I was on my way home to Adelaide and I received a phone call from Jonathan Rose, the Australian media manager at that time, who told me the story was out and I had better get ready for a fiery reception at the Adelaide Airport.

When I got off the plane the place was swarming with press, print journalists, television reporters and cameras. I was asked what had happened. Was the story on the Baggy Green website accurate? I answered that I had in fact used the words printed in the story and I was very apologetic to the players and the team management for any hurt those words had caused.

At the time I thought the best way to handle it was to front up and be honest. There was no use trying to deny having said it; running behind closed doors to avoid people was, I thought, a cop-out.

The story was gaining momentum by the minute; anything in sport that delves into racism or drugs tends to draw world-wide attention and this was certainly no exception.

I knew at this point that there was no way the matter was going to rest. I knew the ICC would step in and take it further and this was highlighted by the comments of its chief executive officer, Malcolm Speed, to the press, prior to any hearing being convened. Speed said he wanted the book thrown at me and made no bones about the fact that if it were up to him I would cop a level-four infringement, which carries with it anything from a ten-match suspension to a life ban.

I was extremely disappointed at Speed's comments. I thought the comments he made in public before the hearing even getting underway may have severely dented my chances of getting a fair hearing.

The head of the body that is conducting a hearing should not pass any comment or judgement on the hearing until it is complete – that's the way *I* thought it worked and I was furious because I believed I'd been drawn and quartered before the hearing even started.

I won't go into the intricacies of the hearing, mainly because there are restrictions on what I can divulge, but suffice it to say it was a very long, involved and drawn-out process. What I will say is that it was an amazing experience. There I was with my legal representative, there was the ICC with its legal people, and the whole thing was being presided over by Clive Lloyd, who has no legal qualifications.

The hearing was conducted just like events in a courtroom. The words used certainly were in keeping with a legal hearing and yet the man who was put in place to make the final judgement was a match referee and former cricketer. The same match referee, I must add, who was presiding over the match in question and the same man who had held the initial meeting in Brisbane and decided the matter was closed. It now didn't seem appropriate that he should have to come back and oversee the full hearing and hand down a completely different and far harsher penalty than he had seen fit to do at the actual time of the incident.

I was charged by the ICC with the offence of having racially abused or vilified an individual. It was an emotional expletive said to myself in the heat of the moment, but something that would never have come out on the ground. I was inside the Australian dressing rooms at the time, My legal team argued that I didn't say anything to anyone's face; I was behind closed doors, and well out of earshot, I thought.

A lot of cricketers have come up to me since the hearing and said they thought it was a disgrace that I could be pinged for saying anything while inside the dressing room. Their point was that the dressing room at a cricket ground is the players' private place and we should be able to say and do what we like while in there, in much the same way people can inside their homes. I am not sure I agree. While I understand their point, what I said was not only wrong but it was said too loudly, and once I realised the people in the other dressing room could hear, it was clear to me that I had a case to answer.

I copped a five-match suspension, just long enough to have some impact on the World Cup, as there were four matches left to play in the Australian one-day international series.

I was pretty angry, I have to say. I was angry that a matter that I thought was handled at the time by the ICC representative on the spot could be re-opened and taken so far. I was angry that the whole thing had used me as an example and I was angry that I was going to miss the next five matches.

I was totally honest right the way through the whole saga. I owned up at the time to saying what I said and I didn't shy away from the Sri Lankan players, who I have a lot of respect for. I fronted them immediately. I was totally upfront and cooperative with Clive Lloyd in the ensuing meeting. I don't know what more I could have done.

It was only when the story made it into the public domain that the ICC decided to have the book thrown at me. Why wasn't it thrown at me on the day it happened, when I was sitting in the room with its representative, Lloyd? If what I did warranted a five-match suspension, why didn't I receive it then and there?

They talked about bringing the game into disrepute, but the way things were handled did far more damage because it was dealt with differently from the way Clive Lloyd initially thought appropriate. After all, the records show that the previous year, when an English player received an equivalent racial slur from a Sri Lankan player on the field, the people in charge thought it fair that the offending player send a letter of apology to the English cricket team. End of story.

I was also disappointed at the lack of support, certainly in the public arena, that I received from Cricket Australia. I am not for a second asking them to condone what I did, but I thought that, I was as one of their employees, they may have been able to state somewhere during the maelstrom that was engulfing me that I was a good person with a pretty good record over fifteen years.

They never said it was totally out of character, nor that I had cooperated fully with all the relevant people associated with the investigation and hearing. I actually had to mount my case with the help of the Australian Cricketers' Association and its chief executive Tim May, who enlisted the help of respected Adelaide lawyer Greg Griffin.

There is a saying in Australia that you 'cop your fair whack' and that was it for me – five matches on the sidelines. It hurt too, missing the finals of the VB Series and the opening match of the World Cup; no sportsman likes to have to sit and watch other people playing the game and that month out of cricket really stung.

One thing that was not reported that day of the hearing, was that it was also our twins' baptism day. It had been planned for many months, and was set to take place in the small church Andrea and I were married in up in the Adelaide Hills. We had invited lots of family and friends to share this special time, many from interstate.

The baptism was booked for early afternoon but the hearing was long and drawn out and, as it went on, it was clear I was not going to make it to the ceremony in time. Andrea, who was already very emotional about the whole ordeal, was frantic as the time passed, really upset that this looked like ruining such an important occasion in our children's lives. She had gone to so much trouble, organised special clothes for the day, and I was not able to be there to help get the kids ready. Instead I had to keep organising to ring her from the hearing and try and give some indication of when I would be out. I had to have my suit delivered to the hotel where the hearing was taking place so I would be able to leave for the church straight away.

Fortunately, Reverend John Stephenson, who has been very supportive to us on a number of occasions, was very considerate. He allowed the ceremony to be put back twice, and explained to our waiting family and friends that we would be along as soon as possible. When we did arrive – separately – Andrea and I both felt upset, yet tried hard to keep this a special day for our children.

It turned out to be the most beautiful ceremony, and extremely grounding on a day like that. I had made a mistake, there was no denying that, and I felt extremely bad. I was also upset by the penalty. It would have been easy on any other day to sit around feeling exceptionally low, but here we were celebrating our twins lives, and surrounded by our closest friends and family. Whilst not wanting to trivialise what I'd done, I was forced to look at the big picture, and felt really humbled. One of the twins' godfathers (and my great mate), Struds, later summed it up perfectly in a speech, pointing out that while it had seemed such a bad day to hold a baptism, it had actually been a blessing that everyone was there surrounding us as a family at such a time. He was right. In hindsight it was the perfect day for a baptism.

If I had my time again I would do so many things differently during this period, but one of the big mistakes I made was allowing myself to be talked into making a statement as soon as the hearing ended.

I didn't want to do it, especially as I was desperate to get to the baptism, and the last thing I felt like doing was a press comment. I also thought I had said all that needed to be said and had been very open with the press. What I should have done is given myself twenty-four hours to gather my thoughts and prepare a proper statement, one that properly reflected how I felt.

I was basically telling a lie in saying I was happy with the sentence and the process that brought about that sentence.

There will be some people reading these words and thinking 'You do the crime, you do the time', and they would be right. I wouldn't have had a five-match suspension to serve if I hadn't said those two words in the first place but it does make me wonder at times.

I wonder what would have happened if I'd lied and denied ever saying it. Sure, I wouldn't have been able to sleep with myself but it would have been my word against theirs and I could have got off.

Still, as a player there is very little you can do. You cop it on the chin and get on with life. Let's be honest, there are worse things that can befall a man in his early thirties than missing a few games of cricket. It pays to keep it all in perspective.

The week after the hearing was tough, especially for Andrea and the kids. We had press photographers following us, a press car positioned at the front of our home and microphones were being thrust in our faces.

It's fair to say there are a few journalists around who, as long as their feet are holding them up, won't be hearing from me again. My rules of handling the media are pretty simple: ask me a question and, if I can, I will answer it. Shoving people aside and confronting me when I cannot comment on an issue is something else altogether.

People often say in these situations 'You find out who your friends are'. I found out that we had lots of really good friends, people who took the time to ring and say they were thinking of us, honest friends who openly said they didn't like what I said, but felt it was totally out of character and that they were there to support us if we needed them.

The Australian players were fantastic. To a man they rallied around Andrea and me and made sure we knew that we had their 100 per cent support, which was great. They moved on to the VB Series finals after the weekend in Adelaide, but they all called during that time and checked that everything was good, which I really appreciated.

The temptation at times like this is to think it will be a slur that stays with you for the rest of your life. You think Sri Lankans will never look you in the eye again and people will be talking behind their hands when you walk into the room.

But the reality is that time heals most things and I have since played cricket in Sri Lanka and the people were wonderful. If you do enough good things in your life, they tend to outweigh the bad in most people's minds. Honestly, if people choose to focus on the one slip-up I've made in a career that's spanned fifteen years, that makes me feel sad, but there isn't much I can do about it.

I learnt a big lesson from this whole unfortunate incident: that the offence I inflicted on the innocent people in the opposition dressing room that day was inexcusable.

TWELVE
ANOTHER FORTY-EIGHT HOURS

There are days, weeks and even months in your life when little out of the ordinary happens. While my life is extremely busy on the cricket circuit, generally it's reasonably predictable. Then there are days when you seem to fit a year of living into forty-eight hours. There were days like that in late February, 2003.

I was in Johannesburg with the Australian cricket team waiting for the World Cup to start the next day. Because I was still serving a five-match suspension, I knew I wasn't playing the next day.

When a cricketer has a day off, the first thing you do is head to the golf course, or go fishing if you are Andrew Symonds, Andy Bichel or Matthew Hayden. I love golf, so on that day I grabbed my clubs and went off with Australian assistant coach Tim Nielsen and selector Andrew Hilditch. We organised a tee time at Royal Johannesburg and set out for what should have been four glorious, uninterrupted hours on a sensational golf course.

That's how it started. We got to about the third tee and all was well. Then Hilditch's mobile phone rang.

Normally mobile phones are banned on the golf course, but

with Andrew being a selector, we thought it was fair enough that he kept his on as the first game against Pakistan was just twenty-four hours away and we hadn't settled on our starting line-up.

As the conversation between Digger and whoever was on the other end of the line continued, I could tell something big was going down. It could have been something in his body language, something he said or perhaps something he didn't say, but I just knew what they were discussing was very serious.

I had known Andrew for fifteen years. He was one of the senior players in the South Australian team when I was first selected and my first room-mate. Add to that the fact that Tim Nielsen, the other golfer that day, had played ninety-nine games for the same state and was a team-mate of mine for the best part of a decade, and you start to realise I was among friends.

So as soon as Digger finished on the phone we didn't hesitate to ask what it was all about. To his credit, he was extremely reluctant to give us any details. The only thing he would say was that it was the biggest thing to happen to the game since Hansie Cronje was exposed for match-fixing. It was going to blow up very shortly, he said.

I immediately pointed out that if it was going to blow up shortly, he might as well tell us now because we weren't in a position to pass it on to anyone out in the middle of a golf course. As hard as Tim and I pressed him, he wouldn't cough up what all the fuss was about. We carried on and by the time we had played nine holes Andrew's phone had rung about fifty times.

At this point he told us he had to take off and attend to this business. To be brutally honest, we weren't overly unhappy to see the back of him. Any man whose mobile rings that often on a golf course quickly becomes unwelcome.

As soon as he left Tim and I looked at each other and asked the obvious question: What the hell was going on? I remember saying: 'It's got to be about one of our guys and, if it's nearly as big as Hansie getting busted, it's got to be about Shane Warne'. Who else could it have been? Warnie was the biggest name in the game and was not a man who shied away from controversy; in fact, it had a habit of following him around.

There was no way I was going to wait until I got back to the team's hotel to find out what was going on, so I pulled my own mobile out and rang our captain, Ricky Ponting, to get to the bottom of it.

'Punter, it's Boof, what the hell is going on?' I asked.

'Warnie tested positive to drugs; looks like he's going home,' came the reply.

I was numb. I couldn't speak. Tim was standing next to me asking what was happening and I just couldn't get the words out. The best bowler in our team – in fact, the best bowler in the world in the past ten years – had failed a drugs test.

I knew Shane Warne extremely well and I equally knew he had the ability to do some outlandish things, things that had often been blown up in the media and landed him in hot water. But taking banned drugs was something entirely different.

The normal questions were racing through my mind: Why would he do it? What sort of drug would he take anyway? He's a cricketer, we don't take performance-enhancing drugs because the game goes for six hours, there's no point.

Tim and I couldn't finish our round of golf quickly enough. Our minds were churning over and we couldn't concentrate.

We headed back to the hotel, totally unprepared for the frenzy that was to follow.

The Australian team that arrived in South Africa for the World Cup was as good as it gets. We were the reigning champions and the favourites to win again, after dominating one-day cricket the world over for the previous four years.

Just weeks earlier we had destroyed England in the finals of the VB Series in Australia after dominating that tournament, which also included former World Cup winner Sri Lanka.

The Australian team was confident and talented. Ricky Ponting was at the helm, having been appointed captain eighteen months earlier. He was already showing signs of growing into a mature and inspirational leader. The 'Fab Four' of Gillespie, McGrath, Lee and Warne were all in career-best form, and the batting line-up included Hayden, Gilchrist, Symonds, Martyn, Bevan and myself. With that amount of talent in a one-day squad, it was no wonder we were pretty much unbackable to win another World Cup.

That was all about to change as we piled into the team room for an emergency meeting on the eve of the tournament opener.

I suspect half the players in the squad already knew what was going on as we headed into that meeting. Certainly the leadership group would have known, as well as a smattering of the senior players. Everyone else was in for a hell of a shock.

We all sat down and Michael Brown, from the Australian Cricket Board, indicated that something had happened and Shane Warne wished to address the group. Shane then stood up to face his fourteen team-mates, the coaches, physiotherapists, team managers, representatives from the board, basically everyone involved in the Australian touring party.

What happened over the next half an hour will never be forgotten by anyone who was there. Warnie told everyone, straight up, that he had undergone a drug test a month earlier, prior to the finals of the VB Series. The results, which had just come in, showed that he had tested positive to a banned diuretic.

You could have heard a butterfly land on the coffee table in middle of the room. No-one knew where to look. Shane suddenly looked every one of his thirty-three years. For a group that's normally so vibrant and happy, this was as low as I had ever seen us. I certainly felt that we would all need to help, not only Shane, but each other, to tackle the intense situation that was about to happen. We needed to stick together.

Shane was emotional as he faced his mates and told us the news. He found it difficult to speak. It's a side of Shane that few people get to see, but I had seen it before and it didn't surprise me at all when he broke down. I have always thought of Shane as a very emotional person. I really felt for him as he faced the room and tried to get the words out.

The thing he was grappling with the most was the fact that he had let us down and he knew it. We were less than a day away from starting the biggest tournament many of us would ever play in and he was delivering the sort of news that could easily derail the whole campaign.

It wasn't good news for him, either. He had retired from one-day international cricket prior to the team leaving for South Africa, so this was to be his one-day swan song.

He apologised to everyone present and said he was sorry for what had occurred and for the timing of the announcement.

But he wanted everyone to know that he wasn't a drug cheat. He explained that the tablet had been given to him by his mum and he had taken it to lose weight. He said it was a vanity issue and had nothing to do with enhancing his performance or injury rehabilitation. I can absolutely say that I believed him.

At this point he broke down for good. That was it, he was cooked. He couldn't finish what he had to say and at that point he left the room. In his wake he left a group of cricketers sitting in stunned silence.

As a member of the Australian team, you sit through hours of team meetings that normally involve departure times, photo shoots, team dinner arrangements and game strategy. This one, as best we knew at that point, had involved the farewell of one of our country's legends, perhaps forever.

What happened then was, to my mind, almost as stunning as what had transpired in the previous fifteen minutes.

Ricky Ponting stood up to address a room that was in tatters. Players didn't know what to think. Was the tournament going to go ahead? Who would be playing for us? What would happen to Shane? What would people say? What would the powers that be do? Many of us were worried about Shane as he went to face the world. In a stupid way the mood in that room was bordering on an emotional Armageddon!

Then, with the sort of forceful resolve that I imagine great politicians and world leaders possess, Ricky Ponting got up and turned the thing on its head. He pointed out, right off the bat that, as sad and tragic as Shane's news was, it had happened and there was nothing anyone in the room could do about it.

That might sound a harsh, even callous thing to say, but he

was right. Shane was gone, and while that didn't mean the team just instantly forgot him, there was nothing any of us could do to bring him back. He was on a flight back to Australia the next morning and we had a date with a fired-up Pakistan team the same day.

Ricky pointed out that, even without Shane, we had the most talented squad in the competition by a mile, and if Shane wasn't able to return whoever the selectors replaced him with would also be a fine player. He said that in a strange way the first match being the next morning was a good thing. Instead of everyone getting embroiled in the inevitable media frenzy, we would all be able to throw ourselves into the first game. Ponting told us that life and the tournament went on and there was no point anyone dwelling on Shane and what was going to happen to him. That would play itself out. If he could come back and join the team, great, but if he couldn't, we must move on.

Cricket is a bit like that. If someone gets dropped or is injured, you feel sorry for them, but minutes later you have mentally moved on to the task at hand. As I said, it sounds brutal for someone as integral to the team and as loved as Shane Warne to be cut off so cleanly by the rest of the team, but as Ricky pointed out, this was something we had to do because we still had World Cup to win.

He also alerted us to the fact that we were down to twelve available players. Warnie was now gone, I was still suspended and Michael Bevan was injured, so for the next day's game we had only twelve players to pick from. It was a simple message and we all understood it clearly. We had been hit by a blow no-one could see coming, but everyone knew what they had to do to turn it around.

We were all sent out of the room with the instruction to go away and think about what had transpired and put together any questions we might have. At nine o'clock that same night we were going to come together again and put the whole thing to bed.

I watched these young team-mates of mine pile out and I noticed that instead of dragging their chins along the ground, they were very much upright. It was still a tight-knit group, as all good teams are. They knew something big had happened but they also knew that something much bigger was starting the next day.

Ricky Ponting's performance in that room was astonishing. That's what leadership is all about and he showed that day that he had what it takes to lead the Australian team.

I went down to have dinner with some of the boys and as we sat at a restaurant in the hotel, it started to sink in that Shane Warne could have played his last game for Australia.

Two hours later we were back in the same room and Shane, after gathering himself together, was able to finish what he wanted to say. He apologised again for letting everyone down and told us he was heading back to Australia the next morning to clear his name. Once that was done, as far as he was concerned, he was going to be back in South Africa to rejoin the team.

After Shane had finished and again left the room, the floor was open for anyone who had any questions. The amazing thing was no-one really did. Ricky's message earlier had answered all questions and from that moment everyone's focus was on the game the next day. Sure, we spoke about it. I certainly did with some of the senior members of the squad and we came up with the same conclusion that most sports lovers did: Why didn't he check?

We all knew that drugs were an issue and we were all given people to contact if we were in any doubt. We have annual education seminars to let us know what's permitted and what's not.

This being the World Cup, the focus was always going to be intense and we knew we would be tested a lot during the tournament. We were all at a loss to work out why Warnie hadn't at least run the tablet past Errol Alcott, our long-time physio.

But he hadn't and the brown stuff well and truly hit the fan, as it was always going to. The media frenzy that descended on Shane the next day was unbelievable. The focus of the world's cricket media was firmly on one man.

Even countries like the United States, which don't care about cricket had flown crews in to try to interview the Aussie who was about to become the first cricketer from that part of the world to be banned for drug use. The scenes outside the team hotel were ridiculous. Cameras, reporters, live-cross vans, helicopters, sirens: it really was like something you would see in a movie.

It was through all of that that we had to make our way onto the team bus and to the ground for the first game of the tournament against the finalist from 1999, Pakistan.

As I said, I wasn't playing that day and neither was Michael Bevan, who had a groin injury. That meant Andrew Symonds was to play in that first game.

If either 'Bevo' or I had been available, Andrew probably wouldn't have been selected and cricket would have missed one of the best one-day innings ever played. Some thought

'Simmo' was fortunate to have been selected on that tour. He hadn't had a great season in Australia and despite having a mountain of ability, really hadn't settled in as an international cricketer. Rumour had it that Ricky Ponting had gone in to bat for him at the selection table. I do not know how true that is, but whatever got him there, it was by the skin of his teeth.

What he did that day against a very good Pakistan attack was resurrect his career and win us the game at the same time. We were in a pile of strife when he came to the wicket, with Haydos, Gilly, 'Marto' and Jimmy Maher back in the rooms. With myself and Michael Bevan out of the team, it would not be immodest to say we didn't have our strongest or most experienced batting group together.

But Andrew climbed into the bowling from ball one, brutalising Akram, Akhtar and Younis to turn a potentially low score into an impregnable one. Watching him blast 143 not out off 125 balls, I thought one career was starting as another ended. It kept flashing through my mind that here was Symonds, after a long time on the fringes, really coming of age and arriving on the world scene with a bang, just as one of our greatest one-day players was departing the same scene by way of a plane back to Australia.

The thing that was most astounding about the innings was that he didn't play like a man with the weight of his career resting on his shoulders. He simply went out there and pasted the bowlers. He was drop-kicking quality fast bowlers over mid-off for six and flat-batting 140-kmh deliveries over mid-wicket for one-bounce fours. He basically hit the ball wherever he wanted. He didn't take his foot off the pedal or show any sign of nerves, even though it could have been the last roll of the dice for him. It was an extraordinary display of power hitting.

He needed it, we certainly needed it, and his team-mates in the dressing room watched in stunned awe. One-day batting doesn't get any better and it was on the biggest stage possible.

There was no-one happier than the skipper. We had been hit by the Warne thing the day before, and at four for 86 we were in real danger of dropping our first game and getting off to the worst possible start. Instead, from the least likely source, the Australian one-day team had again found a way to dig itself out of a hole with aggression and, I think, at the same time rip the heart out of Pakistan. We finished at eight for 310 off fifty overs.

We had beaten Pakistan easily in 1999 and a number of its players were still in the side four years later. To see a good situation turn so bad so quickly must have just about finished them.

Symonds' innings wasn't without controversy, either. Towards the end, Pakistan captain Waqar Younis was removed from the attack at the umpire's insistence for repeatedly bowling 'beam balls'. The removal of a fast bowler from the attack, let alone the captain, for bowling beamers is something I'd never seen happen on a cricket field.

A beam ball is one that doesn't bounce and goes straight past the batsman at head height. It is by far the most dangerous delivery in cricket because as a batsman you are not expecting the ball to be delivered on that trajectory. Your eyes are generally focused much lower trying to pick the ball up out of the sightscreen and off the pitch.

In professional cricket, a batsman will forgive a fast bowler if he bowls one beam ball. Even though you are sceptical, they don't happen often and they can genuinely be a mistake.

But it's inexcusable when a bowler of Waqar's class and experience bowls two. You couldn't blame 'Simmo' for threatening to wrap the bat around his head. As it was, the experienced and respected umpire David Shepherd stepped in, warned Waqar and when it happened again immediately pulled him off.

So we wound up with more than 300 and the boys in the rooms were cock-a-hoop. You don't have to be a cricket historian to know that you don't lose many one-day games defending 310.

Events were to get even stranger because during the Pakistan reply its wicketkeeper, Rashid Latif, was involved in an extraordinary exchange with our keeper Adam Gilchrist.

Gilly said he heard Latif call him a 'white c...'. Adam asked Latif to repeat what he had said and, when the Pakistani player refused, he went to the square leg umpire and formally complained about what he had just been called.

I was watching in the stands and I knew something had been said. And I knew it was something big because Adam Gilchrist is a man I have played a lot of cricket with and against and I know he wouldn't have gone to the umpire unless it was serious.

Given that I had just been suspended for saying something very similar, the issue of racism was fresh in all our minds. In any other circumstances, if Adam Gilchrist had heard those words on a cricket field, he would have ignored them and got on with playing the game. But after I had the book thrown at me, Gilly thought, 'Bugger it, why should Boof be given a five-game holiday and this guy be able to say what he likes and totally get away with it?' On this occasion Gilchrist was incensed with Rashid Latif and he went straight to the umpires with his complaint. He was in no doubt that Latif had uttered those two words.

After the match Adam came and spoke to me about it and I told him that he should be careful opening what really is a can of worms. I asked him if he really wanted to put himself through a hearing and all that went with it. But our vice-captain was adamant that Latif should not be able to get away with saying it and so the hearing went ahead. Rashid Latif denied ever saying the words and the whole issue then came down to Adam's word against his. The case was thrown out.

I was disappointed with some observers, who took a dim view of the way Adam Gilchrist handled that whole situation. There was no doubt in his mind about what had happened and he was only following the laws and the precedent set by the ICC.

What an opening forty-eight hours of the 2003 World Cup!

We had one of the best players in the game thrown out of the tournament after failing a drug test; we saw the emergence of Andrew Symonds with the innings of a lifetime; the captain of one of the tournament fancies was thrown out of a match for dangerous bowling; and the ugly issue of racism flared up again mid-pitch.

After we'd comfortably won the game I sat in the dressing rooms and thought to myself, 'If we can absorb all of that and still beat a side of the quality of Pakistan that easily, there is no-one who can touch us'.

We celebrated heartily that night. It must have had a lot to do with the relief of winning that first game after all that had happened, but we certainly enjoyed ourselves. I remember piling into bed at what must have been about 5a.m. after spending the whole night in a casino and I hadn't even played in the game. It was a lesson we had certainly learnt from 1999. This time the players were determined to celebrate every victory and every great individual performance and that's what we did that night.

The next morning really signalled the end of my 'holiday'. I was playing in the next game in four days' time and in my mind that matched loomed as one of the most important of the tournament. Going into the World Cup, I thought that India was the only team in the competition good enough to beat us. The Indians had big batting weapons and I knew they would be keen to make a statement against the favourites.

It was also my turn to handle the press in the build-up to the game – the Indian journalists were very keen to talk to me about the racism issue. Here was I thinking I could just slide back into the middle order and try to get some runs, but instead I was the spokesperson for the team heading into the game.

What could I have said? I reiterated my statements from a month earlier, that I wasn't proud of what had occurred, and given my time again I would never have said it. I pointed out I had a very good relationship with the Sri Lankan players and I didn't think I was racist.

The writers from the subcontinent had their doubts, but I knew in my heart that I wasn't a racist person and I knew there would be no problems playing against the Indians or any other country for the rest of my career.

But there is no doubt it added some spice to the match against India at Centurion Park, a match which turned into a massive anti-climax, certainly for anyone who had parted with their hard-earned cash to watch the game live. We bowled India out for 125 and got the runs in twenty-two overs. We absolutely decked them and, after that performance, I was even more convinced that we were going to win the World Cup for the second time in a row.

I don't know what it is in sport, but there are times when you just know you have a side's measure and around that tournament, against India, we felt they weren't good enough to beat us. They had awesome talent, so we were always wary, but we knew that if we stuck to our game plan and worked as hard as we always did, we were a better side.

While things were travelling well on the field, off it we were still under siege over the Shane Warne situation. We knew at this stage that he wasn't going to rejoin us – he was out for a year and the reality of a year's cricket without Shane had landed pretty heavily on everyone. The problem was, every time anyone spoke to the press, the first thing we were asked about was Shane Warne and what we thought about his one-year ban, about his taking of the diuretic in the first place, and about his relationship with the team. We were just being asked the same questions and simply wanted to move on.

The senior players in the Australian team are nothing if not honest. I'm talking here about Ricky Ponting, Adam Gilchrist, Glenn McGrath and, I would like to think, myself. When these people were asked about the 'Warne saga', they did what they always did and answered the questions honestly, especially Ricky and Adam. They openly admitted that they thought

Shane had been stupid and they also admitted he had let the team down by allowing this situation to develop to the point where he was banned from the game for a year.

In isolation these comments were fine, because that's genuinely how the senior players in the team felt at the time. We didn't have a personal gripe with Shane but we were pretty pissed off that our best bowler wasn't with us while we were trying to win the World Cup.

The problem arose when Shane, who at this stage was back in Australia, read these comments in the papers and took exception to the words and the perceived undertone of what was reported. I am sure he saw the comments as his mates not being loyal in his time of need, whereas Punter and Gilly were just answering the media's questions honestly.

While I could see how Shane may have taken exception to the stories, I had no problem with what was said because it was the truth, and this was something I told Warnie later on. But let me tell you, there were some moments in the weeks and months that followed where the players concerned in this crossfire were far from comfortable in each other's company. It was stupid, because we're all mates and situations like these can always be sorted with a phone call. That didn't happen, however, and the thing was allowed to fester, which caused something that should have been done and dusted to linger way longer than it should have.

But the great thing about cricket is another game is always just around the corner and that forces you to mentally move on. I had received some text messages from Warnie after we had won and I really appreciated hearing from him. I knew he was hurting and I wished he was there with us, but we had to keep rolling on and even though we had got off to a great start by beating Pakistan and India, we learnt four years earlier that if you take your foot off the pedal in this tournament, you can be sat on your bum very quickly.

THIRTEEN
DEFENDING
THE CROWN

The feeling within the Australian team leading up to 2003 World Cup was a contrast to what we experienced four years earlier in the United Kingdom. This time we were the undisputed kings of one-day cricket and had basically won every trophy on offer. We had beaten every country in a one-day series in the previous four years, so come 2003 in South Africa we were in fear of no-one. We were like Ian Thorpe in the 400-metres freestyle – we only had to be somewhere near our best and there wasn't a team that could come close.

The make-up of the team tells the story simply enough. We had Hayden and Gilchrist opening, followed by Ponting, Martyn, myself, Bevan and Symonds, with Warne, Lee, Gillespie and McGrath. It is hard to imagine a better one-day side in Australia's history.

Of course, when we landed in South Africa we weren't to know that within a fortnight we would be without Shane Warne due to a drugs scandal and Jason Gillespie from injury.

In fact, as documented earlier, the first two weeks of the tournament threw the whole two years of planning on its head. Most cricket followers don't realise that it takes two years to prepare for a World Cup. At least twenty-four months out you start picking the players who you believe will be major contributors come the next tournament.

On the flip side, even if a senior player is still well and truly worth his place in the side, if he isn't likely to still be around at the time of the next World Cup, he will start finding himself on the outer. It sounds harsh, but that's the way it is. You start assembling your group with the sole aim of having it ready when the biggest event in the game begins.

So, here we were, without Shane Warne and Jason Gillespie.

Michael Bevan was also injured and I was still serving the last game of a five-match suspension. So, as good as we thought we were, our depth was severely tested and it was tested right off the bat.

The two things that I believe got us through the first two games and set us on the road to eventual victory were an amazing self-belief that had been built up since the 1999 triumph, and some individual performances from the likes of Andrew Symonds and Andy Bichel that had to be seen to be believed.

One of the great things about having a team that is successful for a long time is that the players on the fringe are desperate to be involved. So desperate that when they get their chance they almost always grab it with both hands and refuse to let go.

The two matches we won to start the 2003 World Cup were some of the best I have ever been involved with, not because they were overly close, but because they showed that, even after being rocked with scandal and injury, we could come out and beat two good sides.

And when I say beat, I should really say smashed. We thumped Pakistan after Andy Symonds' superb century and then we absolutely belted India, who were meant to be one of our major threats.

Those wins sent a clear message to the rest of the teams in the competition. A lot of people had been saying, 'Warnie's not there, let's see how they go now without their match winner'. I don't think they were saying that as we arrived back at our base in Potchefstroom after game two.

Potchefstroom was the best thing that happened to us during the 2003 campaign. It is a small city about an hour out of Johannesburg, the facilities there were sensational, the people were as nice as any you would meet, and it was out of the way. It was basically a big country town. We had the one hotel that was booked out purely for us, there wasn't a massive amount to do, so for us it was perfect and after a while we almost came to think of it as a home away from home.

There were a couple of golf courses there, which is always necessary for an Australian cricket team. The beach was just down the road and Haydos and the rest of the surfers in the team could head there whenever we had spare time. In short, it was the perfect place to set up camp.

There was also a ground in Potchefstroom – we played the Dutch and Namibia there – and the locals almost came to accept us as their own. I am sure if we had played South Africa there they would have been barracking for them but, with the games being against other countries, they were like home fans.

The good thing about a World Cup is the games are quite spread out. You get a lot of down time, time where you are neither playing nor training. This is rare for modern international cricketers. We are normally rushing from one ground to another, in and out of planes and buses, going from airports to grounds to train, and then back the next day to play.

In the World Cup it is not unusual to have a week between matches. For us, that's like a month. Every time we had one of those breaks we would head back to Potchefstroom and relax. Perfect.

The good thing about the games we played in Potchefstroom was the mingling between the teams afterwards. We beat the Netherlands and Namibia very easily, but on both occasions, even before we had finished our warm-downs, they were in to our rooms to have a beer and a chat.

We spent a long time with both teams, talking to their players, giving them tips about training techniques and their games and how they could improve. They absolutely loved it. The feedback we got was that we were the only team that gave them that sort of reception after the game. We were able to do that because we had the time; we didn't have to rush to catch a plane or bus for the next destination. Cricket Australia chose well when they selected Potchefstroom and I imagine it will be used again when Aussie teams tour South Africa.

Aside from Shane Warne, the other big issue to dominate the first half of the World Cup in 2003 was Zimbabwe. The Mugabe regime was attracting headlines right around the world for all the wrong reasons. We heard stories about white farmers being thrown off their properties and people being taken and killed or thrown into prisons. It was pretty ugly.

As cricketers, we were not really in a position to know how much of what we heard was true and, really, it is not our position to stand in judgement. We can have our own private views. Matthew Hayden publicly stated he would not shake

Mugabe's hand if it came to meeting him and a year later Stuart MacGill withdrew from a tour of Zimbabwe because he could not abide what was happening there.

I think it is fair to say most of the Australian cricketers involved in World Cup 2003 had serious issues with playing in Zimbabwe. Even after Cricket Australia put the safety concerns to bed, we were all very uneasy about playing in that part of the world, given what was occurring.

But as a player, you tend to do as you are told. You are selected to play cricket for your country and wherever they send you to play, you pretty much go ahead and play. Sounds ultra-simplistic, I know, but that's how it works and that was the case during the World Cup.

We had discussions about it and players voiced their concerns about safety and the moral question, but we were a team and as a team we were told we were going to play there and play there we did.

As it turned out it was an uneventful experience. We flew in on the day before the game, trained that afternoon, played the next day and flew out that night. We were never worried about our safety. We didn't see anything that resembled a problem during our time there and everyone treated us with gratitude and respect.

We found out later that people who had attempted to protest had been dragged away and dealt with quite severely, which really disturbed and disappointed us. This was kept from us while we were there and to all intents and purposes it was a normal one-day game during that particular World Cup.

We won very easily. Chasing nine for 246, Damien Martyn and I put on 88 and both had unbeaten half-centuries in a seven-wicket win. As soon as the game was over we were on a plane and flying back to Potchefstroom.

I must admit, I wasn't overly happy about going to Zimbabwe at the time. I felt it was the wrong thing to do, but after the game I was very happy we went. We stayed out on the ground after we had won the game and thanked the people who had come and they were very grateful. You could see it in their faces.

I have since spoken to my South Australian team-mate Andy Flower, who says that going there is the best thing to do because it keeps the game alive in that country. Looking back, I have no doubt we did the right thing.

Of course, England withdrew from its match in Zimbabwe and by doing that really made it hard for itself to win the tournament. Similarly, New Zealand didn't do itself any favours by refusing to go to Kenya. I have never been critical of those two countries for taking that stance. It would be hypocritical of me to do so given how close we were to not going, but we did go.

We then went to Port Elizabeth to meet England in our last group game. At this stage we were undefeated. We were coming off three relatively soft games against the Netherlands, Namibia and Zimbabwe, and the clash with England was going to tell us plenty about where our form was.

England is an unpredictable one-day side; it can certainly get hot from time to time. Players you don't expect to step up suddenly find another gear and that makes them hard to prepare for. You pretty much know what you are going to get against teams like New Zealand and South Africa. They will keep coming at you and nine times out of ten they will give an even, consistent, tough performance. With England, you are as likely to beat them by ten wickets as find yourself chasing 290 after their middle order has gone crazy.

As it happened, we were pushed right to the wire and were probably lucky to win. We bowled first and kept England to eight for 204 on a pretty ordinary pitch. We were then in early trouble and it took first Michael Bevan and myself and then Bevo and Andy Bichel to dig in and get us across the line by two wickets.

The funny thing about that game was, as tough a position as we put ourselves in with the bat, I never thought we were going to lose. The confidence we had built up after winning those first two games kept surging through and I always felt we were going to win, even when we were four for 48. Bevan was unbeaten on 74.

From there it was on to the Super Sixes.

We beat Sri Lanka convincingly, with Ponting's 114 off 109 balls leading us to five for 319. The Sri Lankans' reply tailed out at nine for 223.

Then came New Zealand, a team that had played good cricket against us in recent times. Any time Australia plays sport against New Zealand there is plenty on the line – you only have to look at the Bledisloe Cup and the history behind rugby tests between Australia and New Zealand.

We don't particularly like them and they certainly don't like us. When I say we don't like them, I don't mean as individuals, because in that regard they are fine. In fact, I would say that, off the field, we get on better with the Kiwis than most of the other countries. But when it's game time, man, it is on and they do not give an inch.

The beauty of that Super Six series for us was we didn't have to win every game. We'd won so many we only had to win one and lose the other two narrowly and we still would have advanced to the semi-finals.

Turns out we won them all, but the New Zealand match was the tightest of the three. Shane Bond grabbed six for 23 for the Kiwis but Bevan and Bichel supervised our recovery to nine for 208. New Zealand collapsed to be all out for 112 and Brett Lee, with five for 42, was almost as good as Bond.

The other match, against Kenya, brought an easy win, which meant we hit the semi-final stage undefeated. The four teams left in the tournament at that stage were Australia, Kenya, Sri Lanka and India. Kenya had been aided by some teams on its side of the draw electing not to play matches for political reasons. But, to be fair to the Kenyans, they had also played better than anyone expected.

There was some talk about us throwing our last game in the Super Sixes to ensure we met Kenya in the semi-final, the thinking being we would have a guaranteed entry into the final. I can honestly say that was never even discussed. By that stage in the tournament, every Australian player had his eye squarely on winning the World Cup without dropping a match. We honestly thought it didn't matter who we played, we were going to win.

The downside of meeting Sri Lanka was the venue for the match: Port Elizabeth. The pitch there was almost exactly what you find in the subcontinent – it was low and slow and took turn very early. It was completely different to most of the wickets in South Africa, which are very Australian in their style, with good bounce and pace.

The pitch for the semi-final definitely suited Sri Lanka more than us. We batted first and had to work enormously hard to reach seven for 212. Andrew Symonds played probably his most important knock in the green and gold, making 91 not out when the conditions were tough.

Everyone remembers his big century in the first game against Pakistan, but I reckon this was a better innings because it was a far more important game and the conditions were so foreign to him. Remember, he plays in Brisbane, where the ball comes onto the bat and the bounce is considerable. This day at Port Elizabeth the ball was struggling to get above bail height and there was no pace off the pitch at all, yet he worked his arse off to get us to a reasonable total. It was a sensational effort. I got to see a fair bit of it because I made 36 at the other end, and I can assure you, it wasn't easy.

As it turned out, our total was more than enough because Brett Lee bowled one of the most incredible spells of fast bowling I've seen in a one-day game. In the same way that Andrew's innings was awesome, Brett's spell that day was something else because the conditions were so unsuited to pace bowling.

Another big turning point in that game was when Andy Bichel ran out Aravinda De Silva. We had worked hard on our fielding throughout the tournament with our fielding coach Mike Young and when 'Bich' pulled that piece of fielding off it just lifted everyone.

Young was sensational throughout our time in South Africa. He's an infectious American guy who knows plenty about fielding as he has an extensive baseball background. He also has a great way with people. His favourite saying with us was 'take a knee', meaning sit or kneel while he speaks rather than standing up all the time.

So for the whole time during fielding we would all say 'take a knee'. It became the fielding catch cry. But we worked harder on our fielding during those two months than we had for a long time, and it showed. We were pulling off run-outs in every match and the catching was top-shelf, due in no small way to Mike Young's wonderful teaching.

I think the effort we put in that day in the field was near to one-day perfection. There wasn't a mistake made, from the bowlers to the wicketkeeper to the fielders right around the ground. Catches were held, half-chances were taken and the ground fielding was something to behold.

Rain intervened when the Sri Lankans were chasing, but we were awarded the game on the Duckworth-Lewis scale and knew we had won it fair and square. Lee got up some great pace in taking three for 35.

The semi-final was, of course, famous for another incident in what had become a drama-filled event. Adam Gilchrist decided to walk during our innings at Port Elizabeth and in the process opened up a real can of worms. Basically, cricketers haven't walked for twenty years. It was before my time but, as I understand it, the notion of not waiting for the umpire's decision when you had edged the ball to the keeper went out in the late 1970s.

By that point, players were making a career out of the game and they needed to perform to pay the bills. With the stakes raised, giving yourself out became a thing of the past. Players also got tired of being on the receiving end of bad decisions and thought if they got the odd one going their way, it was squaring the ledger.

These days, players will universally wait around until the

umpire gives them out. That was until Gilly took matters into his own hands, in the semi of the World Cup of all matches.

Gilchrist aimed a sweep off Aravinda De Silva and edged the ball onto his pad before it ballooned up into the air. Rudi Koertzen, the umpire officiating at that end, proceeded to shake his head, leaving everyone in no doubt that he didn't think it was out. Then, to the amazement of everyone, including his team-mates in the dressing room, Gilly gave himself out and marched off.

We were stunned: it was the most important game of the tournament so far and Gilly was a reasonably important player for us. He had never spoken to anyone about walking and, to be honest, none of us could believe he did it.

At the time, for purely selfish reasons, we weren't overly impressed. We'd lost our most dangerous batsman when we didn't have to, but afterwards we all understood what Adam had done. I don't think anyone could have predicted the reaction from the cricketing community. Anyone would think Adam had risen from the dead. I don't think he could believe it, either; he was just doing what he thought was right. That's the sort of bloke he is.

To his credit, from that day he has walked every time. He said he would and he has done it and I admire him for that. If he's out, he walks and that's that. There's a lot to like about Adam Gilchrist.

So here we were again in a World Cup final. But unlike four years earlier, where the two matches leading up to the final were some of the most epic ever played in the history of the tournament, this time the lead-in was easy. We had really only been tested twice in the whole thing, once by England in the last of the group matches and then by Sri Lanka for half of the semi-final.

It is fair to say our confidence going into the final was as high as I have experienced with a cricket team. We had India as our opponent, we had beaten them earlier in the tournament and we were very confident that we were going to do the same in Johannesburg.

We had a feeling about India in one-day cricket and that feeling was they couldn't match us in big games. The Indians could in the Test arena – the past two series we have played have underlined that – but in one-day cricket we thought they went missing when the crunch was on.

As we prepared for the final, which was about a week after the semi, we didn't know whether Damien Martyn was going to come up. He had badly broken a finger in his right hand and had been missing for parts of the second half of the tournament. He wasn't sure if he was going to be alright, the doctors weren't sure and, given those facts, the selectors couldn't be sure.

They had told him he would be given every chance to prove his fitness, but his finger was so badly broken that he could hardly hold a bat, let alone use it to any great effect. The medical people were also unhappy about the prospect of giving him any painkilling injections, because he could do real damage and not realise.

So Marto was left to his own devices to work out whether he was confident enough to declare himself fit. What people don't know is that Damien grappled with that decision right up until Ricky went out to toss the coin. He knew he desperately wanted to play, but he didn't want to let his mates down by having to pull out halfway through the match.

Turns out he did play and he turned on one hell of a display. It was one gutsy effort when you think that he missed four months of cricket after the final.

The morning of the final was very overcast and cloudy and we were wondering what to do if we won the toss. Ricky always wanted to bat first – he thought runs on the board were the way to go – and he was very keen to bat first in the final. But with the cloud cover and the threat of rain, it can sometimes work better batting second. You can dictate terms with any run chase where the Duckworth-Lewis becomes a factor.

But the Indians won the toss and took the decision out of Ricky's hands. We saw Sourav Ganguly's decision to bowl as a sign that they were scared of us and it was funny that just as Gilchrist and Hayden were preparing to walk out to the centre at Wanderers, the clouds lifted and the ground was bathed in sunlight. It was quite amazing and sort of summed up the whole two months we had. It was just meant to be.

The first over of that match set the tone for the day. Matty and Adam took to Zaheer Khan, plastering him all over the place and grabbing the initiative from the outset. They had decided to make a stand against Zaheer, because they thought if he copped it early he would drop his head. So they belted 15 off the first over and not only did he drop his head, his ten mates also visibly drooped a little.

The ball actually moved about a fair bit in the first hour of the final, but the Indian bowlers couldn't get the thing into the right place. Instead of using the conditions to put pressure on us, their fielders were picking the ball out of the gutter three times an over.

On reflection, it was really all over after half an hour. The openers intimidated India and laid a foundation that enabled Ricky and Marto to get to work. For a guy who was in grave doubt coming in you wouldn't have known it to watch Martyn that day. Especially in the first hour, he was brilliant. I actually think he out-batted Ricky and that's saying something. He raced to 50 and hit everything right out of the middle of the bat. In the rooms, we didn't care who was getting them. I had the pads on waiting to bat and was happy to enjoy the show.

Ricky Ponting's batting, especially after he reached 50, was as good as you'll see. He hit eight sixes and that's something I still can't believe, a player in a World Cup final clearing the fence so many times. And some of them went a long way – they were seriously long balls. He was just seeing it so well and so early, in the end he was taking the micky. I honestly believe at the end of his innings he was looking around and nominating where the next ball was going to go.

The World Cup has seen some amazing performances and some of those have been in finals, but that knock of 140 not out off 121 balls must rank near the top. It had been a commanding display of captaining right throughout the competition and the innings in the final just capped it all off.

From the thirty-fifth over, we had Andrew Symonds joining me with the pads on. We decided we needed Andrew's hitting ability at the end but we also had to pick the correct bowler. So whoever liked the bowler on at the time more would go in next. In the end we needn't have bothered, because we didn't even get a hit.

When Ponting and Martyn (88 off eighty-four balls) walked off after putting together a partnership of 234, we had two for

359 on the board. It was game over. India was never going to make that many as long as the sun rises from the east.

The lunchbreak wasn't as relaxed as it should have been because the rain that had gone during our innings re-appeared. It wasn't hard but it was there and we were concerned because unless we got to bowl at least twenty-five overs the match would have to be replayed. Not good for us, after making two for 359!

We started perfectly with the ball. Glenn McGrath removed the great Sachin Tendulkar with a skied pull shot and there went India's only realistic chance of winning. We thought that, for them to climb such a run mountain, the little master had to make 150 and even then it would have been a struggle. We'd set them 7.5 runs an over and that takes some doing in any game, let alone a final. We were much more concerned with the weather – after ten overs it was starting to get very dark and on the field we thought it was about to hose down.

So we were faced with a problem. Sehwag was going nuts with the bat at this stage, belting us all over the place, and Ricky was throwing the ball to me and Brad Hogg to try to rip through some overs. He was trying to get us up over the 25-over mark to make it an official game, but little Sehwag was enjoying our bowling indeed.

Thankfully a message came out from the change-rooms that John Buchanan had looked at the weather chart and the band of weather over the ground was only going to stay around for thirty minutes or so. So we came off the ground, had a break and when we came back on went back to our normal set-up, with Bichel and Lee bowling. When I ran out Sehwag with a direct-hit from mid-off and Bichel dismissed Dravid after he dragged one on, it was time to celebrate. We were well and truly home.

The last half of our time in the field was fun. We knew the rain couldn't touch us, we knew the Indians were never going to get anywhere near the total and we just enjoyed ourselves. When I took the catch off Glenn McGrath to end the game, it seemed a matter of seconds before every member of the Australian team, the players who weren't playing, the support staff, everyone, was there in the middle of the ground. It was one big group all piling on top of each other with joy. I don't know how long we were there, but it wasn't long enough.

All the planning, all the hard work, all the scandal and injury, everything had come together and we were again the best team in the world. Not only had we won the World Cup for the second time in a row, we had become the first team to go through the tournament undefeated. I don't think we appreciated it at the time but looking back that was a hell of an achievement. To not lose one game on the way to winning the toughest prize in the game was truly remarkable.

This time in the rooms, we didn't have the manic scenes of four years earlier. I suppose Johannesburg is not quite London, in so much as it's not a celebrity hot spot, so we didn't have the famous faces crowding into the rooms. But one thing that made it really great for me was that Andrea was there. She, Mel Gilchrist and Rianna Ponting were there to watch us win and were invited in to the dressing room.

It was really nice to have Andrea in with me, as she had missed our win in 1999. She always said that if I ever made it to another World Cup final she would be there. It was the first time she had left our young twins, something she found hard to do, but she came for four days and it was very special for us. This time she and I just sat there and enjoyed the moment – a win like that meant as much for her as it did for me. She had put up with a lot over the previous four years and for that moment in the rooms we just sort of soaked it up.

The atmosphere in the rooms that night was sensational. The CD player was booming out songs from Aussie bands like Cold Chisel and Aussie Crawl, every player had a turn at hugging the trophy and we drank far too much.

Again, when the night was drawing to a close we headed out into the centre with the World Cup to sing 'Beneath the Southern Cross'. As we belted out the song, it was throwing down rain and we didn't care because we were on top of the world. Jimmy Maher, who didn't play in the game but was a big part of our touring party because of his general good cheer, did the worm the whole way back to the dressing rooms. The worm is a thing where he sort of 'worms' his way along the ground without actually moving his arms or legs. It's hard to describe but it's unique to 'Mahbo' and hilarious.

Jimmy and I have always hit it off, and together with Ian Harvey we are like the Three Amigos. The laughs always come thick and fast when the three of us are on tour together, and I'm sure we will all still be laughing together in about twenty years' time.

That night we went to a party thrown for us by Travelex, our sponsor, and I am serious when I say absolutely no-one went home. The party went all night and I can't remember one member of the team leaving. The sad thing about winning in 2003 was we only had four days before we had to fly to the West Indies, so the celebrations had to be put on hold a little.

Still, that may have been a good thing because if we were allowed to really let our hair down, who knows where we would have ended up?

It was one of those tournaments where the moons aligned and everything went our way, and that doesn't happen very often. That team and that performance will be spoken about for years to come, I am sure. The World Cup brings the best of the best together and to play as well as we did in that company was something I will never forget.

FOURTEEEN
THE BEST
OF THE BEST

In fifteen years of first-class cricket I have been lucky to play with and against some amazingly good players, players who are the equal of any the game has seen. To watch them up close, either from 22 yards away at the non-striker's end or from 22 yards away while they are trying to wipe you out, is exhilarating.

Add to that the times you are fielding at short-leg watching the world's best batsmen strut their stuff, and there is no better place to witness first-hand the extraordinary talent of some of these players. It sounds corny but I know down the line, when I have moved on and am not playing any more, it will fill me with pride to say, 'I played with/against him' when their names are brought up.

When it's all said and done, that's why you play top-level sport – to pit yourself with and against the very best. Sometimes they are going to get the better of you and sometimes you are going to come out on top and, believe me, when you come out on top against the players I am about to mention (in no particular order), it is the best feeling in the world.

Who are they?

Well, I'm a batsman so we'll talk about them first and it would be un-Australian if I failed to start with one of my team-mates. This guy quite simply defies description, but I'll do my best.

He averages in the mid-50s after playing fifty Tests, he makes his runs at a strike rate of better than 90 and he does it at number seven. He is Adam Gilchrist.

What he has done since coming into Test cricket is remarkable.

The thing I love most about Gilly is the fact that he plays exactly the same way, whether we are five for spit or five for 500. He could just as easily knock the first ball he faces over the fence for six. The same man got off a pair in a Test match in Brisbane by hitting a six. Can you believe that? When we have made a duck in the first innings, most of us gently nudge one into a gap and thank the Lord we haven't bagged the dreaded pair. That's not Gilly's go.

We are talking here about a batsman who can take a Test match away from the opposition in an hour. He can hand the advantage back to Australia inside a session and the other team is powerless to do anything about it.

This is a guy who, coming in at seven can score 50 or 60 in an hour, or a century in a session, and do it in a way that leaves the bowling side devastated. He was once described by the great Michael Holding as a player who leaves the opposition in a 'state of confusion'. I still think that is the best way I have heard his game explained.

You only have to cast your mind back to Gilly's First Test at the Gabba against Pakistan, where the cry was up because home-town hero Ian Healy had been dropped to make way for him. It took just one over, when he hit five fours off Mushtaq Ahmed, for the controversy over Healy to be forgotten. All of a sudden the Australian cricket public thought, 'Wow, we've got an excitement machine here'.

Since his elevation to the top of the order, his batting in one-day cricket has provided the blueprint for the way sides approach the fifty-overs game. He pulls good-length balls for six and hits the opening bowler over mid-on for six in the first over. Give him any width and he murders it. With his unusually high grip on the bat, on his day he's near to unstoppable.

But it's in the Test-match arena where I think he is really something. Test cricket has been going for more than 100 years and it is rare that you can say someone is rewriting the way the game is played. It's usually been done before, somewhere by someone.

But statistics tell us there has never been anyone who has done what Adam Gilchrist is doing. He is a freak. What's the best thing he's done? Hard to say; there have been so many examples. Perhaps the unbeaten 202 against South Africa at Johannesburg in February, 2002, again coming in at number seven, has been his best Test performance. I will never forget watching him charge Jacques Kallis and smack him into the second tier of the Wanderers stand. It was awesome.

The thing about Adam Gilchrist is that he plays with such dash. He bats with a freedom I have never seen in a cricketer before; if it's there he hits it and, believe me, he hits it hard.

The other thing about Adam is that he is becoming a great wicketkeeper in the mould of his predecessors, Rod Marsh and Ian Healy. He has worked so hard on his keeping and his enthusiasm on and off the ground is second to none. To keep to the master, in Shane Warne, is no mean feat but he has just got better and better.

He's a great bloke with it, too – there is no ego attached to him at all. He has a very dry sense of humour and he cares about everyone he plays with and their families.

He is, to put it simply, the most devastating player in world cricket when he's going. When the Gilchrist juices are flowing you take the phone off the hook, lock the front door and sit your arse down on the living room chair. You cannot afford to miss one second.

Next I want to move on to Ricky Ponting.

The second half of his Test career has been exceptional. Again bringing up statistics, something we probably do too often in cricket, his average is over the 50-mark and, like Gilchrist, he scores very quickly, despite batting in the toughest spot in the line-up. Since the big hundred he made against England at Leeds in the 2001 Ashes series, Punter has been the best number three in the world, no doubt in my mind.

What sets him apart?

He can come in at one for 0, the opposition's fastest bowler bounces him and he hooks it ten rows back. He never takes a backward step to anyone, even Shoaib Akhtar, who with Brett Lee is the fastest bowler in the world. Punter still walks at him and still takes him on square of the wicket. That takes enormous talent, guts and a rock-solid belief in yourself.

Having someone like that batting at number three has an amazing influence on the Australian dressing room. Ian Chappell was the same for the great Aussie side in the 1970s. He was a player who went out and attacked the opposition, no matter what the situation of the match. Who can forget 'Chappelli' taking on John Snow of England and hooking him out of the ground?

Like Gilchrist, Ponting changes games and that's what it takes to be included in my list of the best. You have to be able to alter the course of a match with the bat or ball and to do it at first drop, where you regularly have to deal with the new ball and opposition quicks with their tails up, is something special.

My earliest memory of Punter at international level is still my favourite. It's watching him bat with an Australian cap on and taking on the might of the West Indies. Ambrose, Walsh, Bishop – names that inspire fear in most sane batsmen – and here was this kid from Launceston smacking them off his nose. Was it arrogance? Stupidity? I don't know, but that takes some doing and he bats the same way now, only someone's talked some sense into him and he wears a helmet.

The one thing that I know really annoys Ricky is the perception that he isn't as good a player against spin bowling. I don't agree. Anyone who can make a century in Sri Lanka against Murali, probably the best finger spinner the world has seen, can play the slow men.

He's your typical Aussie bloke, Ricky Ponting. He enjoys a punt, loves Australian Rules football and the Kangaroos, and loves playing cricket. His dogs are his other great passion. He owns forty or fifty greyhounds, knows all their names and listens to every race he can, even when we are away.

I would say he's almost bordering on being a 'cricket tragic'. That's a term we use a lot for someone who talks, eats and breathes cricket and never tires of it. He has an enormous amount of fun playing the game, loves playing for his country, hurts deeply when we lose and works as hard on his game as anyone.

The home series against India in 2003–04 was one of the

most amazing batting performances I have seen. To make more than 700 runs in a four-Test series is crazy. He made consecutive double-centuries and he still didn't win the player-of-the-series award. Work that out. When his playing career finishes he will be remembered as one of the best this country has produced.

The next man on my list is heading in the same direction. His career has been staggering, but in a completely different way to Punter and Gilly. Matthew Hayden has become a sensational batsman at the highest level and, believe me, he has earned every bit of success that's come his way.

In a lot of ways his career has followed the same path as mine: he had to wait for a long time to get his crack at the big time. Year after year he made a pile of first-class runs but for a long time found it impossible to break into the Australian Test team. And when he did, in the early 1990s, he broke his thumb and was bounced straight back out of it. So Haydos has had to fight every inch of the way for the privilege of wearing the baggy green.

Matty is a gentle giant and a committed family man. He's a strong Christian and, while he never talks about it much, when you get to know him you are very aware of the strength of his beliefs.

Matthew Hayden most definitely belongs on my list of the best, but if I was putting this list together in the year 2000 he probably wouldn't have been close. But the Test batting he has done since cementing his spot at the top of the order has been unbelievable. Again, and it keeps coming up, his average is comfortably past 50 and like the previous two players he scores his runs at a scary rate.

But to just look at statistics when you're talking about Hayden's batting is to not understand the damage he does to the opposition. Tall and weighing in at almost 100 kilograms, this bloke stands there and just bludgeons the best bowlers in the world. He is so physically powerful and has incredible confidence in his ability to dominate against anyone, anywhere. This amazing self-belief, I think, came out of the series in India in 2001, a series where he had a plan, stuck to it and came away with a huge amount of runs in the toughest conditions the game can throw at you.

His batting during the Ashes series in Australia in 2002–03 was bordering on taking the you know what. Belting Andy Caddick one bounce over his head in the first over, taking Craig White over long on for six – these are quality cricketers and he was treating them like net bowlers.

He doesn't play legitimate cricket shots, like, say, Ricky Ponting or Sachin Tendulkar. His version of an off-drive may not go along the ground – it's just as likely to end up six rows back! You can't begin to understand the impact that has on the opposition bowlers and their captain.

The other thing that's great about Haydos is his love of a confrontation. People watching from the sidelines or on television may not be aware of the rivalry between Matty and Shoaib Akhtar, but I am telling you, when they meet, it's frightening. The big fellow just wants him. He keys himself up for Shoaib and the sparks that fly when they get into the middle resemble the Sydney Harbour Bridge fireworks on New Year's Eve!

When we play against Pakistan, he's like a gladiator in the rooms before we bat. Justin Langer, Wasim Akram and basically anyone else on the field become bit players. It's Hayden against Akhtar and as players we just book our seats and enjoy the show. It's all there: verbal trash, physical exchanges, Matty letting balls hit him and telling Shoaib he's half-baked and asking him when he's going to start bowling properly. It takes a lot of balls to say anything to a guy who can let them go at 160 kmh. But then to keep winding him up so much is bordering on stupidity!

It is on for young and old and the funny thing about it is, if Matty gets through Ahktar's first spell he becomes a 'normal' bloke again, not saying anything, just batting, until the big quick comes back on. Then, bang, they start up again. Test cricket is not always like that. In fact, it rarely is, but when the heat is turned right up, no-one likes being in the kitchen more than Matty Hayden.

I love the big 'Unit', as he is known, and I will tell you why. For years he was unlucky not to be playing regularly for Australia. He put together 1000-run seasons for Queensland – and runs have not always been easy to come by in Brisbane – and yet when others were picked before him, he never complained. He never changed from the friendly, fun-loving bloke he is today, never became bitter like a lot of players who see others getting the glory. Now that he is having his day in the sun, I reckon it's great. It couldn't happen to a nicer bloke.

Moving to other countries, there have been some sensational batsmen in world cricket during my time and the man at the top of the list has to be the prince from the West Indies, Brian Lara.

What a player. Some people may raise an eyebrow at my elevating him to the top of the international list, but there is a clear reason for this – his ability to make runs everywhere. To be the best in this game you have to make runs in all conditions in all countries and Lara has achieved that.

He holds the highest Test score, 400 not out, and the highest first-class score, a staggering 501 not out for Warwickshire against Durham in 1994. How any individual can make 500 off their own bat in any game of cricket is beyond me, let alone in a first-class match.

The Australian players who played in the Test match in Sydney where he made 277 early in his career still talk about it as one of the great innings they have seen. He thought it so good he named his daughter after the city in which the game was played, prompting his team-mates to point out that it was a good thing the match wasn't played in Lahore!

But that is one of Lara's biggest assets. He saves his very best for the matches against Australia and he has played against some very good Australian teams. There have been centuries, double-centuries and Test-winning knocks against the best attack in the world and, unlike previous West Indian greats like Viv Richards, Gordon Greenidge and Clive Lloyd, Brian has done it in a relatively ordinary team.

He has single-handedly won the West Indies Test matches and saved them from losing Test series against Australia, as in the Caribbean in 1998–99. No other player in world cricket can say that.

The other thing that attracts me to Brian Lara is that he's a left-hander like me. It's only natural that I am a fan of the way he goes about it. Why is he so good? He can manipulate the field magnificently because he can hit the ball to any point of the ground and that takes some doing. There are no dud bowlers at the highest level and yet when Lara is on song he makes them all look second-rate.

That said, he has been a little inconsistent. He can come out and just blast, score a century in a session and do it easily, and he can also bat for an hour and not play a shot. Why? You would have to ask him.

The West Indian players tend to be emotional with their cricket and Lara's career certainly has had some ups and downs, on and off the field. But his record stands up against anyone's in the game and, as I said, when he's come to play, it doesn't matter who you are, you will pay.

Brian is a terrific person to play against. I've always found him a friendly guy, helpful and talkative. Despite the reaction some people had to the on-field hostilities in the West Indies in 2003, he's always got on well with the Australian players. We play it hard and he plays it hard. I think he's one of the misunderstood players in world cricket.

He carries the weight of the West Indies on his shoulders and has done for a long time and that can't be easy. Unlike, say, India, where they are united in their fanaticism, the Caribbean countries are notoriously political when it comes to cricket. Lara has had to carry the burden of an under-achieving team while the public in that part of the world still thinks it's the 1980s. He basically can't win when he plays at home. In the First Test of that 2003 series, Lara was booed when he walked out to bat in Guyana. So to carry that around and play as well as he does is amazing.

One of my favourite times with Brian was at the hotel pool after the Guyana Test. We were both, shall we say, enjoying ourselves. I was doing belly flops into the pool and he was carrying on. We were basically misbehaving. Why not? The Test match was over and it was time to let off some steam. I was there with Brian, Michael Clarke and Ricky Ponting. As we were sitting there, the alcohol was starting to talk and Brian turned to me and said, 'Boof, you won't make 50 runs for the series!'

To that point I'd had one hit for six runs, so the way I was going, 50 seemed a long way away. But I wasn't going to admit that to him, so I responded with, 'Bugger off, I'll get 150 next hit, your blokes aren't getting me out!'

I was talking it up by the pool but, don't worry, I needed some runs in that second Test because my career was on the line. He was saying they were going to bounce me and I was gone. These words tend to flow between cricketers when beer is introduced.

Thankfully, I got some runs – 160 – in that next Test. And when I reached 150, the great man slid by me in the field and said, 'Righto, Boof, you've got your 150, now piss off will you? You're ruining the game!'

He's a different character, but lovely to play cricket against and when it comes to wielding the willow, the man is a class act. If he had played for his country in the era when it had the four great quicks, I think people would be speaking about Brian Lara the same way they speak about Viv Richards. Praise doesn't come any higher than that.

Next comes the little master from India, Sachin Tendulkar. He is admired by all in world cricket for two things: sheer weight of runs and his exceptional record against Australia, especially in the subcontinent.

He's a strange player to watch close up. Tendulkar's only a

little man but he's very strong, he uses a massive bat, much heavier than most in the modern game, and he has nothing of the flourish that Brian Lara has made famous. He just picks up the bat, drops it on the line of the ball and most of the time it goes screaming to the rope.

He's an amazing player off his pads, as most Indian players are, and he's a quality player of spin bowling, again as most are from his part of the world. And like all the players on this list he makes his runs in a hurry.

His method of preparing for an opponent is unique. If he's coming up against Australia, he won't do any work against a left-arm finger spinner, for instance, because he knows he's not going to face that type of bowling. When Shane Warne was at the height of his powers in 1998, Sachin got the best leg spinners he could find, flew them all in to Mumbai and faced them for months on end. He had the wickets scuffed up, got them to bowl around the wicket and just worked tirelessly on the skills he knew he needed to conquer Warne. That's what I call leaving no stone unturned, and when that series came around, he dominated Shane. In fact, he was the first batsman in world cricket to completely disarm the great leg spinner, for that series anyway.

The only chink in his armour is that he has struggled at times with the bounce in Australia. When you use a heavy bat and you play the ball on line rather than length, you often find bounce a problem, especially at places like Perth and Brisbane when it's delivered by tall men like Glenn McGrath and Jason Gillespie.

Sachin is not on his own with this dilemma. Many great Indian batsmen have found the going tougher in Australia, the reason being that the conditions are so totally different. The ball stays new for longer in Australia because the pitches and the outfields have more grass and the ball bounces more off our tracks.

The highest compliment you can pay Sachin is this: you have to remove him to beat India. No matter what else is happening in the game, he is the one you must dismiss to get on top of them. He is an intimidating player whose presence at the crease totally changes the context of any game he's playing.

Sachin Tendulkar as a man is almost unlike any other superstar I have met, in my sport or any other. He is quiet and reserved, which might come from the almost deadening weight of expectation he carries around with him, especially at home. I would almost feel confident in saying never has a cricketer been lauded so much by his own people. In India, especially in Mumbai, Sachin Tendulkar is beyond royalty.

He once purchased a Porsche sports car, a GT3, one of the fastest production cars in the world at the time. The problem was that he could only drive it at 3 a.m. because the crush of people any other time when they realise it's him behind the wheel wouldn't allow him to get out of first gear.

When he's at home he can't leave his house and when he's playing in another city in India he can't leave his hotel room. When he goes to the movies in his home town, he's got to go in disguise, otherwise he would be mobbed to the point where he wouldn't see the show.

I have always got on well with Sachin. We share the honour of having been at Yorkshire as overseas players and when we speak that's pretty much always what it's about. He will ask me how the various players are going, his old mates.

He's probably at his happiest in the middle, where he can weave his special brand of magic. When he does, you just sit back in awe.

The third of my internationals may surprise a few, but this player has surprised me with the massive leap he's made into cricketing stardom. I speak of Yorkshire's and England's Michael Vaughan.

I first saw him at Yorkshire when I was there as the overseas professional and during that time I witnessed the most amazing transformation. When I first went to Leeds, Michael was a stodgy opening batsman who actually resembled that other famous stodgy Yorkshireman, Geoff Boycott. He had all the shots in the nets but he just wouldn't play them in the centre.

At Headingley, where the wicket does a bit, I remember him coming to me once and saying, 'Boofa, I'm batting a full session and making 20, what's going on?' Basically here was a guy who worked his bum off to stay at the crease in difficult circumstances but he wasn't reaping the rewards.

What I told him was pretty blunt: 'Start playing a few shots!' I told him he had the weapons – I'd seen him display them in the nets and it was time he started playing them out in the middle. My message was if you're going to make 20, you might as well make them in half an hour and get the next bloke in. Taking a whole session to put 20 together wasn't helping anyone. It certainly wasn't helping Yorkshire win too many games. He always looked a million dollars at the crease, but at that time his cricket was stagnant.

Well, I am not sure whether it was me or whether he made the decision for himself, but that was the end of the Geoff Boycott impersonations. The next phase of his career for

Yorkshire and then England was quite something.

Michael worked out that, as an opener, he had the best chance of attacking the opposition because the field was always up. In Test cricket especially, you always get at least three slips and a gully to start with and that means there have to be some gaps out there. 'Vaughny' started pounding the ball into those gaps.

He basically got himself out of that very Yorkshire mould of being technically correct at the expense of making runs and started playing the way a player of his talent should. He took the 2002–03 series in Australia apart. Against a very good team he cracked three centuries and 633 runs, being named player of the series in a four–one loss!

I can't remember an opener playing McGrath, Lee and Gillespie the way Vaughan did that summer. At times he was treating them with contempt, pulling them through mid-wicket off the front foot – and these are balls coming through at 150 kmh. Driving on the rise, cutting … dare I say it, he was batting like an Aussie. And even though I was on the opposite team, it was awesome to watch.

He makes his way in onto this list on the back of two years of outstanding Test match batting and, a bit like Matty Hayden, an ability to completely turn his career around. He's gone from being a good first-class player to an exceptional Test player quite quickly and he's been playing in an ordinary England side for most of that time.

He's also a typical Yorkshireman, amazingly tight with his cash. I have never seen him buy a drink. You would think now that he's England's skipper he might dive into his pocket every now and then but, no, he's just the same. Perhaps the captain's allowance, if they still have such a thing, will turn him around. But I never miss him at the bar and I am not going to start now.

Still, he can play and if England is to become a force in world cricket, it will do it on the back of this guy. I reckon he's that good.

Michael Vaughan rounds out the best six batsmen I have seen in my time. This isn't about picking a team, but imagine trying to bowl those six out. You'd want to do it quickly, otherwise they'd make 600 in a day!

To win any Test match you need to bowl a side out twice and that's why the bowlers are the most important members of a team. As a batsman it hurts me to say that but let's face facts. If you can't bowl the opposition out you won't win too many games.

Recently Australia has won plenty of games. It holds the record for the most Test-match victories in a row and the past three captains have all retired with sensational win–loss ratios, mostly on the back of one man.

Shane Warne.

Earlier I spoke about Adam Gilchrist completely re-inventing the way the game is played. Shane Warne has been doing that for a decade. He's the most dynamic cricketer I have seen, a player who has won more games off his own back than any other I have witnessed.

How many times in his long Test career has Australia been deep in the brown stuff, staring at defeat, only for Warnie to take three quick wickets and turn the whole game around?

Traditionally the role of a leg spinner in cricket was to remove the tailenders, who were generally mesmerised by the ball spinning above their eyes. Shane got rid of them, don't worry, but he got rid of numbers one to six as well and he removed them when they were generally well set.

In terms of cricket, I grew up with Shane Warne. We played with and against each other a lot in our early years and when he was young the amount of spin he put on the ball was outrageous. He was incredible. No-one had ever seen a leggie turn the ball that far and with so much control. He bowled flat, hard, huge-turning leg breaks that would land on a twenty-cent piece. Try scoring off them – just staying in was difficult enough! Most of the time you just battened down the hatches and tried to do your scoring at the other end.

Generally you saw bowlers with control but not a lot of turn, like Anil Kumble, or you saw them turn it but cough up a lot of hittable balls. Warnie never gave you anything to hit and he had variety – he bowled flippers, zooters, wrong 'uns, straight ones and drifters, and he landed them all right on the spot.

But more than that, he's been a big-time bowler. He loves the big stage; he thrives on it. The bigger the occasion, the better he performs and when Australia's back was against the wall, Border, Taylor and Waugh time and again threw the ball to Warne, and time and again the blond bombshell delivered. High-quality batsmen cruising in their innings on a flat track … bang, Shane would have them, then he'd have a couple of their mates and the whole game would change.

The 'Gatting Ball', as it's become known, his first delivery on English soil in a Test match, has to be the ball of the century. In a warm-up game Warnie was belted for plenty by Graeme Hick at Worcestershire. Allan Border, the Aussie captain, had instructed him to bowl nothing but leg spinners and keep the rest of his tricks in his kit bag. How clever was that? Then along came that ball.

It was the moment he became a household name in every cricket-playing nation.

Shane has lived a Hollywood lifestyle, but he and I are good friends – we are because he's a genuinely nice bloke. If Shane Warne likes you, you'll receive plenty of support from him.

He's amazingly generous when it comes to charities. During his year away from cricket with the drug ban he took a group of terminally ill kids to the United States for the trip of a lifetime. He has set up his own foundation to help the underprivileged and he regularly supports charities with private funds when he can't physically attend.

In the second half of his career he has changed enormously as a bowler, basically because he had to. Injuries first to his finger and then to his shoulder have made him change the way he goes about his craft. He can't spin the ball as hard as he used to, so he's tightened his control even more and brought the back-spinner into his armoury. That's given him a lot of lbw decisions and in a lot of ways he's become a better bowler.

It's a bit like the great Dennis Lillee, who injured his back and had to stop being a tearaway quick and learn to swing and cut the ball. Shane re-invented himself and in my mind that makes him even greater. What a record: more than 500 Test wickets and more than 100 Test appearances. Leg-spin bowling is the most difficult skill in the game of cricket by a mile – that's why so few of them are ever successful.

Shane is also an amazing presence on the field. When he first played against Chris Cairns, the big New Zealander, like many before him, really didn't have much of an idea about Warnie.

When Cairns came to the crease in a Test match at the Gabba, the Australian captain, Mark Taylor, said to Shane: 'Let's get a couple under his nose at short leg and silly mid-off, he won't last long'.

'Yeah, Tub, let's do that in a minute,' Shane replied. 'I just want to humiliate him for a while!'

This is happening in a Test match!

But that's the way Shane thinks: he has amazing levels of confidence and he almost always backs it up.

Cairns, by the way, learnt quickly, because in future series he played very well against Warnie and made good runs against Australia.

No leggie in the game has ever come close to having Shane Warne's impact, on or off the field, and I have always thought it a privilege to play with him and the toughest test in the game is to play against him.

Put simply, he's the best I have ever seen.

The other spin bowler who has rewritten the record books in modern times is Sri Lanka's Muttiah Muralitharan. This is a man who before he finishes will, in my opinion, have broken every wicket-taking record in the game.

He is a sensational little bloke; one of the nicest international players I have ever come across. He always has a smile on his face and he always plays attacking cricket. Whenever I face Murali, I know it's 'game on'. He is trying to get you out with every ball and therefore you are given the chance to score. That makes for really entertaining cricket.

His fields are usually attacking and he bowls a line that allows you to score, as much as it gives him the best chance to get you out. The subcontinent, Murali's home turf, is often the most difficult place for him to bowl because the wickets turn that much he damn near has to land it off the cut surface to threaten the stumps.

The 'revs' he puts on the ball are outrageous. When it comes out of the hand you are intimidated by the amount the ball is spinning. He spins it almost as hard as Warnie did and that's not comparing apples with apples, because a finger spinner never spins it as hard as a leg spinner ... well, not until this bloke came along.

The other thing that makes playing against Murali nearly impossible is you have no idea how far the ball is going to turn. They all look to be spinning with the same ferocity, but one ball will spin a bat width and the next will spin three feet.

The only saving grace for me with Murali is that he doesn't bowl anywhere near as well to left-handers. When he is in top form, bowling over the wicket to right-handed batsmen, he only needs a couple of fielders on the off-side because the ball is spinning so hard from outside the off stump that it's almost impossible to score through the areas like cover and point. But lefties like me have the ball turning away from us and we get the odd one to blast away when he over-pitches or drops short.

As for the one that goes the other way, the 'doosra' as people call it, I actually found it quite easy to pick in Sri Lanka in 2004, especially after I'd been facing him for a while. The ball is pretty much bowled with the same action but instead of it turning from off to leg, this one spins like a leggie, back into the left-hander and, more dangerously, away from the right-hander. But I found that while the ball was in the air, you could see it spinning in the other direction if you looked hard enough and that gave the secret away.

Murali has much to be proud of and he is a proud man. He is Sri Lanka's first superstar cricketer and one of the best.

The West Indies have had many superstars and many of them have been fast bowlers. For a while it was like a production line … Roberts, Holding, Garner, Marshall, Croft, Walsh – the list just rolled on.

Thankfully, I never had to face a lot of those players but the best in my time, by the length of the straight, was Curtly Ambrose. He was genuinely fast, frighteningly fast, and he let them go from nine foot-plus!

Tall men like Curtly and, I suspect, Joel Garner before him, are rarely acknowledged as being superfast. Because the ball tends to bounce so much they don't look like they are getting it through as fast as the smaller guys. But players who faced Garner assure me he was right up there with the quickest when he wanted to be and I guarantee you Ambrose was as well.

But pace was only one of his assets, and he had plenty. This bloke was a mean fast bowler, not mean-spirited – he actually always struck me as a very gentle, shy person – but mean in a competitive sense.

When you were out there facing Ambrose you were the enemy and he wanted to get you out, either dismiss you or knock you out, it didn't seem to matter. He was like a pitbull terrier with a bone in its mouth.

The worst thing about facing Ambrose was he never gave you anything to hit. His line and length were unbelievably good and because he was so tall there was really very little you could do about it. He was very tough to play horizontal bat shots against because he never gave you enough room to cut and the ball was rarely short enough to pull.

I am not too proud to admit it – there were times when facing this massive West Indian was genuinely frightening. You were dead-set fearing for your safety and any batsman who says otherwise is either naïve or lying!

What in God's name was Steve Waugh thinking in the Caribbean series in 1995 when he told him to get back to his mark and bowl? And I have no idea why Dean Jones would even think about asking him to remove the sweat bands in Sydney. These are crazy men with a deathwish!

I was always as nice as possible to the big man, who in turn very rarely said anything and that made him all the more scary. On the morning of a game against the West Indies, when some of his team-mates would say hello, Curtly would just look, nod and walk away.

I started playing regular international cricket just as he was finishing, thankfully, although I did play against him a fair bit playing County cricket in England and you earned your money every time. There was never an easy game against a team with Curtly Ambrose in it.

Back in the early 1990s, when he was at his peak, he was the best fast bowler in the game and I have to say I didn't lose one second of sleep when the big man decided to retire in 2000.

Pakistan's 'Rawalpindi Express', Shoaib Akhtar, gets a mention in this list purely because it's impossible to bowl the cricket ball any faster than he does. They say Jeff Thomson was the fastest ever. Well, I am sorry, 'Thommo', but I just can't believe anyone has bowled faster than this bloke. He was once clocked at 160 kmh and that's just a ridiculous pace.

Shoaib is extremely difficult to face because he has a strange action that doesn't allow you to get a good sighter on the ball.

Brett Lee, who is also exceptionally fast, has such a clean action that you see the ball clearly out of his hand. But Akhtar has this windmill-style delivery and you only see the pill as it's hurtling towards you, pretty much making a bad situation a lot worse.

He loves the big stage, Shoaib. The bigger the crowd and the better the opposition, the more he enjoys it. He's a showman, a lair, an entertainer and an excitement machine all wrapped in one package.

Nothing excites a crowd more than seeing an express bowler strutting his stuff. I don't know what it is but there is something about raw pace that gets everyone sitting on the edge of their seats. Adam Gilchrist once said that a ball bowled by Shoaib to him in a one-day match in Bristol hit the stumps before he had the chance to start his downswing! Now that's quick!

The only good thing you can say about Akhtar from a batsman's point of view is that he's never held that pace over his whole spell. You knew that five overs in, the pace will start to drop off and that's when you get some balls to hit. When he gets tired his accuracy also starts to fall away. But it's been a matter of surviving long enough to get to that part of his spell.

Shoaib Akhtar is great for the game. When you face him your heart races, the adrenaline starts pouring through your veins and when he winds it up, especially in Pakistan with hundreds of thousands of fans screaming, there isn't a more exhilarating experience to be had in the game.

I'm staying in that part of the world for the most complete fast bowler I have seen.

Wasim Akram had the lot.

He was fast enough, though without being at Akhtar's level,

he swung the new and old ball both ways, he would bowl over the wicket, round the wicket, short run, full run, it didn't matter … it was all superb.

The great Greg Chappell, one of the best batsmen the game has seen, is on record as saying the one bowler he is glad he missed facing was Wasim Akram. That is not something you hear very often, because past greats generally like to think they could handle whatever the modern game serves up. But Greg saw what I experienced and that is a bowler who, at his top, did not have a weakness. He would bowl all day, lively pitch or flat, and it didn't matter if the opposition was one for 10 or one for 200.

Wasim pioneered and perfected the art of swinging the old ball. The thing that made him such a difficult bowler to counter was that he could hoop the ball both ways and he swung it so late he made you play at every ball. Halfway down you weren't sure whether it was going to come back into you or tail away. When you consider you have less than half a second of reaction time when facing a fast bowler, it doesn't give you long to make your decision.

He pretty much won Pakistan the World Cup in 1992 when he came on and knocked over England's middle order in a devastating spell of one-day bowling.

A deceptively tall man, who was always very easygoing, he was brought through the Pakistan system under the guidance of Imran Khan and there was some of Imran's swagger about Wasim. But that was only in appearance. He was a very humble man but on the field he was there to get you out, nothing more.

If I were selecting a team to play for my life Wasim Akram

would open the bowling, no question. He's the best and most complete fast bowler I've put eyes on.

Finishing closer to home – and this guy is very close to home; he plays club cricket about five minutes away from where I live in Adelaide – Jason Gillespie is a man I love and admire. I've watched him develop from a young bowler in his teens who used to come down to the SACA nets and bowl for hours to the State team, to the most feared fast bowler in Australia. When I say feared, I don't mean physically, although 'Dizzy' (after the jazz musician) can bowl very fast. I mean feared as a bowler capable of getting you out with every ball.

Like Wasim Akram, he is a lot taller than people think and with that height comes a very awkward trajectory. Gillespie uses that trajectory differently to, say, Ambrose and someone like Glenn McGrath: he bowls a lot fuller than those two. He tries to hit the top of off stump, whereas Glenn's stock ball is clearing off stump by a foot. Because he pitches the ball up more he can go for more runs, especially when he's bowling to four slips, a gully and a bat-pad, but in my opinion he's also far more likely to get you out.

Dizzy's strike rate at Test level is up there with the best to have played the game and this is what a lot of people who don't know much about cricket don't understand. The bowling statistic that interests captains and coaches much more than average is strike rate, because that tells you how often a bowler actually gets someone out. There's no point bowling economically if you never dismiss anyone and with Jason Gillespie that's what he attempts with every delivery.

He's also a lot quicker than he looks. Now that speed guns are being used you can see he regularly ticks over 140 kmh and that is fast enough. In his early twenties he could at times be express – just ask Justin Langer, who had his hand broken in three different places by Gillespie in one of the fastest overs ever bowled at the WACA ground in Perth. And it wasn't as if Justin wasn't seeing them too well, either: he was 200 not out at the time.

Dizzy is one of those bowlers who tends to bowl within himself until the conditions are right. Then he turns it up and, when he does, look out. The seam of the ball after it leaves his hand is almost always gun-barrel straight and the area he gets the ball going through when he's on song is tough to handle. It's basically working a right-handed batsman over by getting the ball passing through about roll-of-the-pad height, just on or about off stump.

Alec Stewart, the very good and experienced English keeper–batsman, always said he was the Aussie quick the Poms least liked to face. That's where you really find out about a player, by asking the opposition.

He bowls a very good bouncer as well, which is something you can say about all the fast bowlers I have mentioned. Gillespie rarely wastes a bouncer; when he decides to bowl one it is generally right on the button.

But the thing I love the most about him is he is so attacking. He never tries to protect his average, never wants fields that will give him protection. He tries to take a wicket with every ball. That makes him a delight to play with and to captain on the rare occasions when we've got him back to play for South Australia.

He's a sensational bloke, a guy who has been dealt some horrendous injury cards in his time, but he has never dwelt on it.

He has missed almost as many Test matches as he's played and the figures show if he had played in those games he would have been up there, statistically, with the best the game has seen.

No matter where the cricket gods have taken Dizzy he has remained the same. You could run into him after he's taken seven wickets in a Test match, or leaving the doctor's surgery after another scan, and I guarantee he will treat you with the same amount of courtesy and respect. It's impossible to find anyone with a bad word to say about him. I may be biased, but when he's fit and bowling well, he's as good as it gets.

Wouldn't you love to see that attack bowling at the six batsmen I spoke about earlier? You couldn't find a ground with enough seats.

The two areas of the game I haven't mentioned are wicketkeeping and fielding.

The best wicketkeeper I've seen standing up to the stumps was Jack Russell from England. He's also the most unusual man I have come across in the game, bar none. You can't go to his house in Bristol without wearing a blindfold because he doesn't want anyone to know where he lives.

He taped up the same pair of gloves and has done since he first started playing. The quality of wicketkeeping gloves has come along in leaps and bounds during Jack's time in the game, but he kept taping up the same pair.

But his glovework was outrageously good, especially when he was standing over the sticks. You see the keepers in the modern game standing up to medium pace and sometimes fast bowlers in one-day cricket. Jack Russell used to do it regularly in four-day cricket and probably bagged himself another 100 dismissals because of it.

When Australia's Ian Harvey was the professional at Gloucestershire, they had the leg-side stumping down to such a fine art that they used to manufacture two a game. You don't see his quickness of hands behind the stumps very often. He generated two or three chances per innings by doing things other keepers wouldn't consider and that is a special gift.

Standing back, the Australian keepers are the best in the world by a long way, probably because they get so much practice from such a young age. The pitches in Australia generally carry through nicely, even in junior cricket, so our keepers are brought up standing back.

I think the other thing that makes Australian glovemen so good off the faster bowlers is their focus on footwork. The great Rod Marsh, who was before my time, had sensational footwork and therefore his keeping looked effortless. I think that's his legacy to the Australian game.

Ian Healy is the best I've played with and against. He was a workman at his trade. He got the best out of every piece of ability he had and he improved right through until the day he retired. I always say the yardstick of a good wicketkeeper standing back is the amount of catches he drops, and I genuinely can't remember 'Heals' dropping more than two or three. I am sure he spilt more than that in his career, but if he dropped more than one in a series you couldn't believe it. He held on to everything.

Ditto for Jamie Siddons, the best fieldsman I've seen. Sadly, injury cut down the amount of work he was able to do in the in-field. In the end he was basically restricted to fielding in the slips, but when he was younger his work in the covers was simply awesome. Diving full length, throwing in the same motion, hitting the stumps from side on while in mid-air, he could do the lot.

But it was his catching that was truly amazing. I played with Jamie for South Australia for a long time and I only ever saw him drop one catch, and that was when he was the substitute fieldsman. He had beautiful soft hands, as all good catchers have, and he had great anticipation – he would seem to start diving for the ball before the batsman had even edged it. He reacted quicker than anyone around him and he used to make catches happen.

Against Tasmania on the fourth day of a Sheffield Shield game the opposition was trying desperately to hold on for a draw. Tassie all-rounder Shaun Young was blocking hell out of Tim May so Jamie went and stood at silly mid-off, pretty much with his left foot on the pitch. As Young blocked the ball he jumped forward and took the catch off the face of the bat. I've never seen anything like it and that's why I put him just ahead of Mark Waugh, who was also a great fielder.

FIFTEEN
MY MATE
HOOKESY

The tragic passing of my good friend David Hookes happened as this book was being written. While this chapter appears late in the text, many of the references to David earlier in the book were penned while he was still alive.

I was with David at the Beaconsfield Hotel in Melbourne on 18 January 2004. A short time later I was just metres away from him when his head hit the pavement and his fight for life began. I was also there as the heartbreaking decision was made at the Alfred Hospital to turn off life support.

That night I not only lost one of my closest friends, I also lost a fair bit of the innocence that I was unaware I possessed.

David and I had been friends since the day I first walked into the South Australian dressing room as a seventeen-year-old, in 1987. He was the South Australian captain at the time and by far the biggest presence in cricket in my home state. That he welcomed me immediately into the fold when others may not have been afforded that warmth perhaps comes down to the similarity in our backgrounds.

We both came from hard-working homes and neighbourhoods and it's fair to say we both weren't overly keen on any 'airs and graces'. Hookesy called a spade a spade and so did I. He liked players who had a go and didn't die wondering; that was certainly right up my alley. He was a left-hander, as am I.

I found him approachable and supportive and never had

any problem playing cricket with him and under his leadership. In hindsight, I couldn't have had a better captain when I was starting off. He taught me right from wrong on and off the field, but he never tried to curb my natural style and he never tried to change me as a player or a person. I loved him for that and, even after I went to Victoria, a move he criticised me for at the time, he remained a valued friend and mentor.

Few people ever realised how much I lent on David, even when we were playing for different States. He was always only a phone call away and when I was going through some tough times in Melbourne, David would often pick up the phone and just ask how I was going. He told me to stick at it, he reminded me that I had the ability and assured me that it would all be fine in the end, and that's exactly the sort of help you need when you are in your early twenties.

Even when Hookesy finished playing and moved into the media, a line of work where relationships with players can often break down, he remained firmly in my corner. When he moved to Melbourne and started working with Gerard Healy on 3AW, I would speak to him perhaps once a week, and our relationship turned from being one of mentor–student to very close friends.

I am not saying he was a father figure or the biggest thing in my life or any of the things you sometimes hear said in these situations. He was simply a bloody great mate who always had time for a chat and was never shy in offering his advice and support if he felt I needed it.

Earlier in the day, before we found ourselves at that St Kilda hotel, David and I had done battle in a one-day game at the MCG, he as the coach of the Victorian Bushrangers and me as the captain of the South Australian Redbacks. It was a good game, tightly fought, and, as happened far too often that season, my team ended up on the wrong side of the result.

But as David had taught me during my time in his team, win, lose or draw you catch up for a drink afterwards and we were always going to have a beer, regardless of the result.

After the day's play Wayne Phillips, a great mate of David's, our physiotherapist John Porter, and I had organised to meet Hooksey, Vics captain Darren Berry and a few other senior staff from Victoria at the Beaconsfield Hotel on Beaconsfield Parade, St Kilda.

The night unfolded like a thousand other nights we had together over the years. We stood at the bar, having a couple of beers, and we talked in a relaxed fashion as we kept an eye on the one-day international that was being played between Australia and India on the big screen.

What happened in the next hours was a tragedy. There is no other way to describe it. I am unable to go into any detail about the events of that evening as the criminal law courts are still to deal with the matter.

Actually, it suits me not to write about the details of the incident. From a personal perspective, it's something I think is best left unsaid. I will never be able to erase the memory of what occurred outside the Beaconsfield Hotel on the night of 18 January. I have often heard people say that everything happens for a reason, but the harder I try the more impossible it has been to find any good reason for David's passing. He should still be with us and he isn't, and as best as I can work out, there is no good reason for that.

All I remember after the incident had occurred was just standing there, numb to what was going on around me, looking at Hookesy in the hands of John Porter and having the sinking feeling that something really bad was happening.

David had basically stopped breathing and even after the ambulance arrived they continued with CPR for what seemed like an eternity, trying to keep him with us. The longer the treatment went on the more it dawned on me that Hookesy was in real trouble. I don't know much about the medical profession, but I was pretty confident that a man who needed to be helped to breathe for half an hour after being knocked unconscious was in a bad way.

They couldn't get him into the ambulance to get him to hospital because he wasn't responding to any of the treatment from the paramedics. Eventually they stabilised him enough to get him into the ambulance and off we all headed to the Alfred Hospital.

I was there with Wayne Phillips, Darren Berry and Victorian fast bowler Michael Lewis. We joined David's wife Robyn and other close friends who went to hospital on hearing the news.

What followed were some of the most tortured hours you could ever imagine. David was clearly in a lot of trouble, but we didn't know exactly how much trouble at that stage and we had the onerous task of ringing the people closest to him to tell them what was happening.

As we were sitting in Emergency, the doctor finally came in to tell us what was going on. I started to leave, as did the rest of the people there who weren't family, but Robyn asked that we all remain with her. She didn't want anyone there to have to leave, so we stayed.

The doctor looked us in the eye and told us that David was not going to survive. I went cold. I just could not believe what I was hearing. I expected the doctor to tell us that even though he was in a bad way, he would eventually pull through. The last thing any of us thought he would say was that this was the end.

I kept thinking, 'This can't be happening. I was standing next to this bloke at the bar just hours ago and now I'm being told that it's all over'.

Robyn was obviously in shock and there was a group of his best mates doing it just as tough as I was. It was a surreal situation and one it took me a long time to grasp.

One of the hardest tasks I had to perform that day was to ring members of David's family. I had to call his children, Kristofer and Caprice, his brother Trevor, in Queensland, and Ian Chappell, one of his longest-standing cricket mates.

How do you ring people in the middle of the night and tell them news like that? It was horrendous. The basic message was to drop everything and get to Melbourne because David was in hospital and in big trouble.

Everyone there was given a task, some people to ring and, as hard as those phone calls were to make, in a strange way they kept us focused on a job at hand rather than sitting there thinking about what we had just seen and heard.

About 5 a.m. David was moved from the Accident and Emergency Department to Intensive Care. By this time a lot of people had begun to arrive. A lot of his friends and work colleagues who had been alerted to the situation had made their way in and at this stage I decided it was time to head back to the hotel.

It was a very strange situation. There was one of my best mates in a hospital bed on life support with nursing and medical staff working around him. To the uneducated eye he looked fine. He looked like he was going to wake up any minute. He had a bit of swelling on his face but otherwise he looked like he was asleep.

As I made my way back to the South Australian team hotel I couldn't come to terms with the fact that it was all over. I kept thinking some sort of miracle would occur and he would wake up or, if not wake up, perhaps the doctors would revisit their initial diagnosis and give us some glimmer of hope. That, of course, was just my inability to understand and deal with the truth as it was laid before me. David was gone and I knew he was, even if a large part of me refused to accept it.

As I lay in bed at the hotel I drifted off into a very ordinary brand of sleep, the type where I suppose you are sleeping but you are aware of everything that's going on around you. Then the phone started to ring and it didn't stop for two hours until I finally had it taken off the hook. My mates, David's mates, our former team-mates, everyone under the sun rang to find out what had happened. I guess word had got out that I was there and most people knew I was a good mate of Hookesy's, so I was the logical man to call.

The phone pretty much continued to ring for two days. In the end it all got too much and I handed the baton over to Greg Blewett, the South Australian vice-captain. He became the spokesman and he was sensational; he was a mate of David's and although he hadn't been there on the night he knew I was a long way from being able to speak about it. He handled the press and the public and did it amazingly well, because he would have been feeling bad too.

That enabled me to go back to the hospital on the second night and say goodbye to my great mate.

Tuesday night, two days after the incident, it was clear that

David's life support was about to be turned off. The organ donor people had been consulted and the correct procedures had been put in place and it was time for him to go.

Wayne Phillips and I went back to the hospital late on Tuesday night, which became early Wednesday morning. While we didn't say it to each other, we both knew we were there to farewell our friend. When we arrived, David's family was there, together with Shane Warne, Paul Nobes and Darren Berry. It was, as you can imagine, very quiet and sombre. Even though it was now some forty-eight hours since we first arrived at the hospital, I still couldn't believe what had happened.

Slowly, one by one the people there said their personal good-byes to David, in their own way and in their own words.

I don't know why but I just couldn't leave. I tried to muster the courage to say what I knew I needed to say, but I couldn't do it.

I remember sitting at David's side for twenty minutes, maybe longer, just talking to him, as if he was fully listening. Perhaps he was. I was telling him everything I wanted to say but in no particular order. I don't know if it made sense and I don't even remember what I said. But it felt better saying it.

I told him I loved him and I told him I would never forget what he had done for me. I said if there was anything I could do to help or protect those he loved, I would do it until it was my turn to move on.

He was just resting there, a perfectly normal-looking Hookesy, a calm expression on his face as if he was in the middle of a peaceful sleep. By this stage the bruising around his eye had grown into a bit of a shiner, but otherwise he looked, as I said, just fine.

That, I think, made it tougher to come to terms with, and I was already doing it tough enough. You know those times when you know you need to say goodbye but the words just won't come out? Well, this was one of those times.

I could almost hear Hookesy saying to me, 'For Christ's sake, Boof, get it out'. Man, what I would have given to hear those words from him.

I kissed him and whispered goodbye and squeezed his hand for a second and told him I was going to miss him. Then I got up and walked out. At this stage I was just numb; I knew I would never see my great mate again and I knew within hours he would be announced dead. I couldn't face up to either fact.

Walking out of that room, I can still hear the doors close behind me, the hospital doors. The sound comes back to me all the time, as clear as a bell. That was it, it was all over, and that sound signified that it was done.

I hugged Robyn and the kids, who I know were in so much pain and yet showed such strength at the time, and then I left them to their own goodbyes as I headed out into the night. It was without doubt the hardest thing I had ever had to do.

So many thoughts were whirring through my head. I had lost a dear friend. I had the man who was alleged to have done it in my head. I kept thinking about him, the bouncer. I knew he would have to deal with his own set of circumstances. But all I could think was: 'Why? How did it end up this way?'

I guess the correct way to describe my roller-coaster of emotions over those three days was shock. I was genuinely in shock. I didn't know what time it was or what day it was. Half the time I didn't even know who was talking to me. I was pretty much walking around in a daze and nothing was making much sense.

I have since taken counselling on how to deal with these situations and a lot of what has been said to me has made a great deal of sense.

One of the things I haven't been able to do, however, is return to the hotel, even though the counsellor suggests it would be a good thing. I just can't do it, not yet. Maybe one day I will be able to go back there and perhaps I will get some closure from that.

What I also wasn't ready to do was play cricket, even though we had a four-day game scheduled for the end of the week against Victoria. Clearly, nobody was ready to play cricket, not us or the Vics, and the correct decision was made by Cricket Australia to postpone the game.

At this time playing cricket again seemed a long way away. I just didn't care, didn't care if I ever picked up a bat again, didn't care if I played for Australia again. I basically didn't want to know about the game.

Of course, I have since returned to playing cricket, as David would have demanded, but it's funny, every time I bat I think about what happened. Every time, without fail. I don't know why it happens. Sometimes it hits me just as the bowler is about to let the ball go. When I look up to the scoreboard, I just see David and remember what happened.

Certainly as a captain now I am always thinking, 'What would Hookesy do if he was here?' I find myself constantly thinking about him, not in a sad way. He is just there and I am now very used to him being there.

I have found it very tough to sleep since David's death. I wake up in a cold sweat most nights and that's generally the end of my sleep for the evening. I can't go to nightclubs or pubs any more without feeling nervous and vulnerable.

It is getting better with time, but that constant, nagging feeling that everything isn't right has been with me ever since that night in St Kilda. I can be sitting somewhere alone and the whole thing will come flooding back to me and I will just break down. Something inside me says I am weak and I start telling myself to get over it and move on but I can't. I just have no control over it. The whole incident shook me up much more than I ever thought it could.

On the Saturday night prior to the funeral on Tuesday I was asked to speak to the Australian players, who were in Adelaide for the one-day internationals that weekend. They wanted to know what had happened and I guess find out how I was going, along with their other mates in the South Australian and Victorian teams. I found it a good thing to have done. I spoke to them about the night and about the ensuing couple of days. Some wanted the full story, others just wanted to know how I was, but it was good to talk about it. It actually struck me that I hadn't really spoken to anyone in any detail about it since it happened.

I have to admit, the funeral was something I wasn't looking forward to. The day of the funeral was staggering. Some 15,000 people attended the service at the Adelaide Oval and the outpouring of emotion was quite simply amazing.

Andrea and I were honoured to be part of the family group on the day. We took our places out on the oval and as I looked back I could see the grandstands groaning with people. In a way it was fitting, because when David was flying out in the middle, with his Gray-Nicolls bat in hand, the stands were equally full of people who just loved to watch him bat.

On the day of the funeral the South Australian Cricket Association had paid David a fitting and very poignant tribute by leaning one of his old bats up against the stumps with his SACA cap hanging off the bails and his gloves nearby. Anyone who knew Hookesy knew that was how he left his batting gear at a drinks or tea break. He did it all the time and it was great to see it again.

Probably only a small percentage of the people there that day understood what it meant. But the players who played with and against him knew and we all appreciated it. I actually thought I was going okay at the funeral until David's coffin came through the gates. Then my emotional floodgates well and truly opened. Just to be at that famous ground where I had shared so many great hours in the middle with Hookesy and then seeing his coffin in the back of a silver car ... it was all too much. I remember I had tears rolling down my face. I don't know how long I had been crying because I am not sure when they started or ended.

The actual running of the day was superb. The speakers all did a sensational job and the courage of the people entrusted with those roles, from David's family members and close friends to Ian Chappell and Wayne Phillips, was inspiring.

To speak so personally and lovingly about someone who meant so much to you and not break down was amazing to me. I am sure I wouldn't have been able to do it, but they all did and each did a wonderful job of providing some peace and hope to us all. There were also a few laughs, which Hookesy would have loved.

The attendance in the marquee afterwards and then at the Queens Head, a pub over the road from the ground, was equally amazing. The crowd was a who's who of world cricket. Players from Test nations right around the world were there, old and young, to pay tribute.

It was a warm feeling to see all these old mates and drink a beer to one of our own who had meant so much to each and every one of us. I saw Dennis Lillee talking to Clive Lloyd at one stage and the great Richie Benaud was there, as were South Australian players past and present. It was a great cricket gathering.

That's the sort of game cricket is. You play hard on the ground but after hours you forge lasting friendships and David Hookes had obviously done plenty of that, if this group was anything to go by.

It was an amazing, surreal day. David Hookes had returned one last time to light up the Adelaide Oval, this time not with his flashing strokeplay but with his mere presence. Everyone was touched by it.

I will always remember Hookesy for the way he tucked me under his considerable arm right from the start and kept me there for twenty years. He protected me and guided me in a way I will never be able to thank him for.

The thing I loved about Hookesy was that he never asked for anything in return for all the phone calls he made to ask if I was alright; for all the faxes and letters of encouragement when things weren't going well; for the congratulations when things did go well; for the barbecues at his and Robyn's place; for the beer after the game; and for the tickets to the football. For everything he did so selflessly for me, he never once asked for anything back.

I never did get to properly say thank you to Hookesy for any of that and now that he's gone I never will. All I can do is take his lead and provide those under me with the same care and support that he showed me. If I manage to give any young person half of what David Hookes gave me I will be a very proud man.

I was asked to write a tribute to David for the *Sunday Mail* in Adelaide. I wasn't really sure I wanted to at first, but once I sat down and wrote it I was really glad I did. This is what I wrote:

A Tribute to My Childhood Hero

In 1977 at the age of seven during World Series cricket, I found my first hero. A young and brilliantly talented cricketer by the name of David William Hookes, or Hookesy as I have known him for all these years.

Who can forget those great moments that he had on the cricket field. The five fours off Tony Greig. The sixes off Andy Roberts after coming back from a broken jaw. His brilliant hundred against the Vics, and many more. He was truly amazing and captured my imagination. As a kid I hoped to be just like him one day.

He was everything that I loved. A great entertainer, a brilliant captain and a person who never took a backward step.

As one of the great mentors in my career, I look back now and realise that I have embraced many of the traits and principles that David taught me. He gave me a firm belief in my own ability, and little did I know he was nurturing me to become the person and the player that I am today. I hope that my achievements are something that he could have been proud of.

Over the last few days I have been through lots of emotional ups and downs, but trying to always focus on the good times as much as possible.

David has always been a close friend and confidant. If I had a problem he would be one of the first people I would call upon for advice and guidance.

We would spend hours passionately talking about life, cricket and sport over a beer or two. I learnt so much from those conversations over the years. I loved to hear him talk about all my childhood heroes and tell me stories of years gone by. We both had strong opinions – mostly because that's the way he taught me to be. He would never give in if he thought he was right and nor would I. Together we loved it!

I owe so much to David and his family for all they did for me along the way and the values they instilled in me. A firm belief to tell it how it is and go with my gut instincts on the field as a player and a captain, but also in life in general. Treat everyone as you would like to be treated. Always respect the game of cricket, and those who helped and supported you to where you are today.

There is nothing more sure than this fact, the senseless death of David Hookes has left the world a poorer place for us, and there is a massive hole in my heart. I am left with fond memories of a man I idolised for many years and still do to this day. The past week has been one of the most traumatic times in my life as well as for my family. But when you sit down and think how much pain Robyn and her family would be feeling right now, they are the ones who have lost far more than us. They have lost a husband, *a father, a brother. My thoughts are with them at this time and always will be.*

The cricket world is in mourning and I can only say to all these people that Hookesy would want us to remember the good times and move on with our lives as much as possible. He always lived life to the fullest and we should heed his example. Go for your dreams in life and achieve them. 'Do what it takes' – I can hear him now from above.

I am going to miss you mate. You helped make me the person I am today. I think about you every moment of the day and want you back. I know this can't happen, so we all must get on with things, just as we know you would expect. I know that the pain will go away at some stage, but I will never forget you and what impact you had on my life. As people read this I hope that they will remember the man, the legend, the controversial character, the captain, the media personality and that young man that changed our lives for the better. But there won't be a moment, each time I walk out on to Adelaide Oval, that I won't be thinking of you.

P.S. Your legend will live on in us all and we will remember you. Please don't forget us, as there is no bloody way I could ever forget you. Rest in peace my friend. Love you mate, Darren.

SIXTEEN
SRI LANKA:
THE ULTIMATE TEST

O n the eve of the Test series I was nervous about my comeback. I was unsure if I had the strength, emotionally and physically, to overcome the turmoil that had been swirling all around me and to get back into the game after all that had happened.

A few months earlier I had injured my Achilles tendon, to the extent where a surgeon told me if I kept playing for much longer it would definitely snap.

And during this time I suffered the loss of my mate David Hookes. His death deeply affected my state of mind; I had never faced anything as devastating in my life and found it desperately difficult to cope.

But it's amazing how life works. After a horrendous six months during which I lost one of my best mates and was seriously injured for the first time in my career, the place I went to resurrect my career was Sri Lanka.

As I embarked on the series, a small knot of anticipation growing in my stomach, I knew little of what would unfold over those first few days. What an emotional release it turned out to be.

Sri Lanka is a special place for me; it is where I played my first international for Australia in 1996. It is also a particularly beautiful country with its beaches, stunning rainforests and friendly, laidback nature. The people are always welcoming and treat us well when we tour.

Sri Lanka is not as intense in its love of cricket as, say, India, where you can never escape the fans' crushing passion for the game. In hotels and restaurants, they wait by the hundreds. They know everything about you as a player and can rattle off all your statistics. In Sri Lanka – and this is not to say that people aren't interested – it's just not the be-all and end-all.

You only have to look at the attendances at the Test matches. When we were there they had the best Test-playing nation the world had seen since the mid-1980s, it was a ripping series, and yet hardly anyone came. I'm not sure why, but they are different to the crowds at home and in most other countries.

But the lack of people didn't bother us one bit. We were there to win, which was always going to be difficult; on their own soil the Sri Lankans are an extraordinarily tough team to beat. They play well in their conditions and they have at their disposal the greatest finger spin bowler the game has seen: Muttiah Muralitharan.

In hindsight, I couldn't have picked a better place to make my return to Test cricket. While the cricket was always intense on the field, the place itself is very relaxed and low key, and the focus is not on you twenty-four hours a day, which is exactly what I needed. I was able to play the games hard, then disappear into my hotel room and wind down without having to attend functions or catch up with friends. Importantly, I didn't have everyone constantly reminding me of what had happened in the previous few months.

It was an important tour for me. I hadn't played for Australia since the Second Test against Zimbabwe at the start of the Australian summer and it really was make-or-break time. When you're in your thirties and playing Test cricket for Australia, you can't afford too many bad games because there are outstanding players outside the team waiting for their opportunity.

The other big problem I faced was the uncertainty of picking Muralitharan. I had, of course, faced Murali before but I had never seen the mysterious 'doosra', the ball that spins the opposite way to his stock off-spinner. Given that I had missed the one-day tournament, it was looking like I'd be heading into the First Test without even a glimpse of the little magician.

There was no doubt this was going to be a major hurdle. I have always been a very good player of spin bowling – I've never lost much sleep over facing it – but Murali is a completely different kettle of fish. He can humiliate the best players in the world.

Having said that, I felt in great form going into the first lead-up game of the tour. I had made a double-century against New South Wales in Sydney just before leaving, with Stuart MacGill part of the opposition's attack. I felt I couldn't have had a better test, making runs against a fine spinner on a turning surface.

I got to that first match in a different frame of mind. My attitude towards life, let alone cricket, had changed dramatically since Hookesy's death. After that, cricket seemed not so important to me as it had been. I now realised that if I was lucky enough to once again be playing for Australia, then I was going to try to enjoy every moment. I know Hookesy would have expected that of me. My whole aim going into Sri Lanka was to enjoy myself and enjoy the game of cricket.

The tour got off to a perfect start for me. I made a century in that lead-up game and I tried a few risky things in the process. I started standing off the wicket to the spinners, giving them a clean view of all three stumps. I wanted to send a clear message to the spin bowlers: I was on the way and I was going to come after them – they weren't going to dictate the terms to me. If they wanted to prepare turning wickets like that, I would play my way.

I reverse swept when I was only on 15, something I never do. I ran down the wicket and slogged them straight back over their heads, stood off the wicket and banged them through extra cover.

I certainly enjoyed the tour match, which is something you can't always say. They can often be tedious affairs played against substandard opposition in pretty ordinary conditions, but for me it was all about getting back out there with the green and gold on and having fun. And with that game under my belt it was time to turn my attention to the First Test in Galle and my meeting with the great Murali.

The Australian team going into that match had a very different feel about it, the obvious reason being the new captain, Ricky Ponting. Steve Waugh had led the side for some eight years and a successful skipper generally moulds the side around him. The team is run exactly how the captain wants and that's precisely how it should be – it's his team. Steve had his way, which we had all become used to, but now that he was gone we had a whole new set of parameters to adjust to with Ricky in charge.

For those of us who had played both forms of the game the transition was relatively easy because we had already seen how Ricky went about running the team. But for players like Justin Langer, who plays only in the Test team, it must have felt a little strange.

Ricky and I have always been pretty close. I have enormous respect for him as a player and I really admire the way he leads the Australian team, especially in adversity, as we saw in South Africa prior to the World Cup in 2003.

Anyone can be in charge and ride the wave of success when things are going well; the real test of a leader is how he handles a situation when the wheels start to come off. In South Africa, Ricky showed that he was a leader of the highest order.

I like to think he also enjoyed having me around. A captain at first-class level and at thirty-four, I've played a lot of cricket. He knew that while I wouldn't bombard him with my ideas, if he asked for my thoughts I would tell him straight. It's funny, there were times during the series when Ricky would ask me about a bowling change or a move in the field, and I got the feeling he already knew what he was going to do but just wanted it confirmed. Even though I never spoke to him about it, I felt he liked having another shoulder to lean on every now and then. I'm honoured that my opinion is sometimes sought. Of course, he does the same thing with the likes of Adam Gilchrist and Shane Warne, and this is one of the real strengths of the Australian team. There are so many experienced players and it's great to have so many qualified opinions to draw on.

On the day of the First Test I woke and straightaway was

nervous. That's not entirely unusual for me; I am always a little toey, especially before a Test match. But this time I was more nervous, because I hadn't been in the Test arena for five months and I didn't know how the Murali meeting was going to go. And I hadn't fully tested my emotional resolve, if you like, since the passing of Hookesy.

We won the toss and elected to bat. As a batsman you always want to bat first, no matter what the conditions or the opposition are like. I was down to bat at number five and I was almost straight in as we lost three wickets quickly. It was perfect from my point of view. While not great from a team perspective, when you go in early you don't have time to get anxious. You just go through your routine of getting ready to bat and when the wicket falls you are out there.

I vividly remember walking to the crease. And, amazingly enough, the bowler I faced was Murali. There was no waiting around to see if I was going to pass that test – this was sink or swim. The first ball he bowled to me was the big off-spinner, which I had seen plenty of times.

The second ball was the doosra. I was amazed by how much it spun the other way. But once I had seen it a few times, I felt confident in my ability to pick it. At this point I felt my nerves subsiding and I started to feel good. I was back and doing what felt natural. I sensed the pressure lifting and I felt sure I was going to make runs. Sounds strange, I know, but, given the quality of the opposition, this is a feeling that doesn't come over you very often as a Test cricketer

So from early in my innings I felt calm. I believed the other Sri Lankan bowlers weren't going to get me out and the big danger wasn't as big as I had anticipated. Some people thought

I was rolling the dice by hitting Murali back over his head so early in the innings, and the truth is there *was* a bit of bravado involved, but I was also picking him very easily out of the hand and in the air, so it was not as big a risk as people perceived.

I made 63 before Murali bowled me around my legs. It was my own fault; I got too smart and wandered across my stumps. I still can't believe I didn't get some bat on it but as disappointing as it was to be dismissed, I was back in the baggy green and I had batted well.

Right throughout that innings, and I batted for a good four hours, I felt in control. For the first time in my Test career, I felt I was actually controlling the game, not sitting back and making my contribution while someone else dominated. It was a great feeling.

The same thing happened in the second innings. After Matty Hayden had made a great hundred, Damien Martyn and I came together and again I felt we were totally driving the game. I couldn't believe the fields the Sri Lankans were employing. There I was, fresh at the crease, with Murali turning the ball square, and yet they were rarely using close catchers. Even if you made an error of judgement and got a little edge on to your pad, there was no fielder in there to take the catch. They were strange tactics. The Sri Lankans hate going for runs, so as a batsman you know if you can get a few through the gaps and start to put the pressure back on them, they will turn defensive very quickly and make batting so much easier.

The other thing about my batting in this series that seemed to amaze people was my footwork. I was batting a long way outside leg stump one ball, then outside off stump the next.

One ball I would walk down the wicket and the next I would play right back. A lot of people, some of them in my own team, were at a loss to work out what I was trying to do.

Though I was surprising a fair few people with some of my shots, I have played that way against spinners for years. The main reason for it is to change the field, something all bowlers, but especially spinners, hate. By batting outside leg stump you can work balls on middle and off stump through extra cover for a single. And by moving across outside the off stump you can work the same ball through mid-wicket. Nothing infuriates a bowler or a captain more than having their field manipulated.

Okay, sometimes it doesn't work , as we saw in the first innings in Galle when I possibly cost myself a century, but over the series it worked a treat. I think I really unsettled the Sri Lankan spinners, especially Muralitharan, who I doubt had ever seen it done before.

If the Sri Lankans thought I wasn't going to sweep and went without a fielder at backward square, I would sweep to get a fielder moved there, and so create a gap somewhere else in the field. It's all about making the bowler bowl to you. That's how you control the game and when you do, you invariably make runs.

The advantage for us on this tour was that the ball was spinning so far you couldn't get out LBW. Unless you were right back on your stumps and hit below the roll of the pad, it was virtually impossible to be adjudged leg before.

Take that mode of dismissal out of a spin bowler's armoury and he has to work out a new way of dismissing you. It's tougher to bowl to a player who isn't worried about getting out LBW and, with no close-in catchers, the equation was really starting to suit our game.

Damien Martyn and I capitalised on the great start from Haydos and it was awesome to share a big partnership with Marto, as he was also under intense pressure coming into the series. He had struggled in the one-day matches during the Australian summer and his Test series against India, while being far from ordinary, was not up to his high standards. As I have said, this is a tough team to stay in and he needed some runs, as much to convince himself as anyone else that he could still get the job done.

Marto is great. He plays the game the way it should be played: with freedom and style. He hits the ball so hard, but with what seems very little effort. He picks the bat up, drops it on the ball and it goes screaming away, normally through point and extra cover, his favourite scoring area. He's not an overly demonstrative cricketer; he's a bit like Mark Waugh in that he lets his play do the talking.

Despite all the pressure on him in the build-up to the Galle Test, Marto batted superbly and from twenty-two yards away I was pumped that he answered his critics so emphatically.

While he was playing so well, I was also inching my way towards the three-figure mark and that was enormously satisfying after batting well in the first innings. Marto got to his century just before me and I ran down and hugged him because I knew how much it meant to him and how important it was for the side.

When my turn came, I was overjoyed. It had been an incredibly difficult period of my life, but I had somehow come through. The emotion I felt when I reached my century was overwhelming. It was my comeback Test match.

As the ball went to the fence I felt a massive weight lift off my shoulders. All the crap I had waded through in the past five months was gone and I lifted my eyes and my arms to the heavens and said a silent thanks to my great friend David Hookes, who had died less than three months earlier. I knew he had been looking after me.

When I had got into the 90s I started to think about what a century would mean. I began to think about what it meant to be back in the Aussie team; what it would mean to Hookesy, who made his only Test hundred in Sri Lanka; and what it would mean to family and friends who had stuck by me through the tough times. I started to get excited.

When the 100 came, I was totally overcome with emotion. I simply grabbed Damien Martyn and couldn't let go. I don't know what I said and I don't remember what he said, but I just clung on to him with tears rolling down my face. The relief of the moment was overwhelming and I was very glad Marto was there to hold me up.

It may sound strange, but I firmly believe Hookesy was there during the early part of the Sri Lankan tour. It was as if he was watching over me and making sure I was okay, because he would have known how tough I had been doing it. I didn't 'speak' to him or have some out-of-body experience; I simply got this warm feeling that he was with me. So when I brought up the century in the second innings and looked up in thanks, it was as though he looked down and said in his typical manner, 'You're right now mate, you don't need me any more, off you go, get on with it'.

Oh but I needed him. There were times during the tour

where I could easily have packed my bags and gone home. There were nights in the hotel room where I would sit alone and cry. I was really struggling to come to terms with the fact that he wasn't around any more.

The worst time was after the Test win in Kandy, where David had made his only Test hundred. All the boys were in the rooms whooping and hollering, as we do when we win, but I sat out the front in the viewing area on my own. I could almost see him batting out there, with the baggy green on that funny angle on his head, taking the ball off the stumps through mid-wicket in true Hookesy fashion. A steady stream of tears flowed down my face. I wasn't sobbing but they just kept on coming and I welcomed them.

The boys came out from time to time, offering me a beer, making sure I was okay, but they knew why I was out there and they knew I wanted to be alone to reflect on recent events and try to get some closure after such a difficult time.

I had long chats with Adam Gilchrist and Ricky Ponting about how I was feeling and they were fantastic. They supported me 100 per cent and their message was compassionate and simple: they both said that there has to be a point where you move on. I did want to move on, but grief is a tough thing to control and just when you think you are getting ahead of it something shakes you.

Gilly and I had a big night on the drink in Kandy and that was great. I hadn't been to a bar or a nightclub since the night it all happened; I just didn't feel comfortable or safe. But Gilly took me under his wing and we had a great time. I suppose it was all part of the healing process.

I didn't feel completely normal until the halfway point of the

Third and last Test. That's when I started to feel like the me of old, not anxious, not worried, without a knot in my stomach, not fearful without knowing why.

All the way through the Sri Lankan tour the thing that made me feel good was simply playing cricket again. It was my escape: it was the place where I could forget about everything and just be me. I suppose you could call it a sanctuary. I felt best when I was out on the field playing the game I loved.

The other exceptional thing about the Sri Lankan tour was Shane Warne's return to the Australian team.

Warnie's bowling performances in those three Test matches had to be seen to be believed, and reaffirmed his greatness. To take twenty-seven wickets in three Tests despite not having played an international match for twelve months was extraordinary. To dominate the series and lead Australia to a three–nil win was outrageous.

Even more than the wickets he took, for me it was the manner in which he took them. We were seeing the Warnie of old: shape was back on his leg breaks, the loop and drop, the drift to leg, the bounce and sharp turn. When he is bowling like that he will always get wickets, especially when the surface is turning, as it was in Sri Lanka.

Sri Lankan batsmen are generally very good players of the turning ball – they see leg spin regularly and on their own tracks they play it well. For Shane to dominate a series on their soil was some achievement.

The difference between Shane and Murali, both great bowlers, is that Shane regularly dismisses the opposition's top six; he doesn't rely on tailenders to get his wicket tally up. That is not a criticism of Murali, because one of the prime jobs of a great spinner is to remove tailenders, who generally have no idea how to handle the turning ball. But Shane has never feasted on the batting bunnies. He gets front-rank players out and he gets them out when they are set. That, in my opinion, sets him apart from any other spin bowler I have seen.

In this series he took nearly half the wickets on offer and he bowled us to victory in the process. To be there and see his resurrection was a privilege. Even in the Third Test, when he was seriously tired after carrying the load in the previous two matches, he still wanted the ball and he still wanted to win. That is why he is a champion.

The best thing for me was watching him on the last day of a Test trying to win the match, nostrils flared at the scent of victory. Warnie had that zest back; he was enjoying the game, he was laughing a lot, having fun with his team-mates. It reminded me so much of the Shane Warne I saw come into the game a decade earlier.

Walking out of the ground after the match at Kandy, Shane turned and thanked me for all my support over the past year. He's not normally given to saying things like that, but he showed then that he valued the help of those around him. For him to say that to me was greatly appreciated.

In fact, Warnie's attitude summed up whole tour: everyone had fun. Justin Langer took over the singing of 'Beneath the Southern Cross' and he was like a little kid in a lolly shop. Punter was loving being in charge and getting his new team across the line. Every player chipped in at one stage or another with the bat or ball and it was a really harmonious tour.

The teams got on extremely well. I don't remember a cross word on or off the field; the matches were played in the correct spirit and the Sri Lankan players, even though they lost three tight, tough Tests, carried themselves with class and dignity.

The tour gave me the feeling of achievement I had been striving for in my cricket career. I finally felt I belonged in the Australian cricket team; I had shown that I was capable of making a significant contribution to a winning side and no longer felt on the periphery. Also, I felt that the emotional roller-coaster I had been on might finally be slowing and I started to feel some closure about recent events. I looked forward to the future.

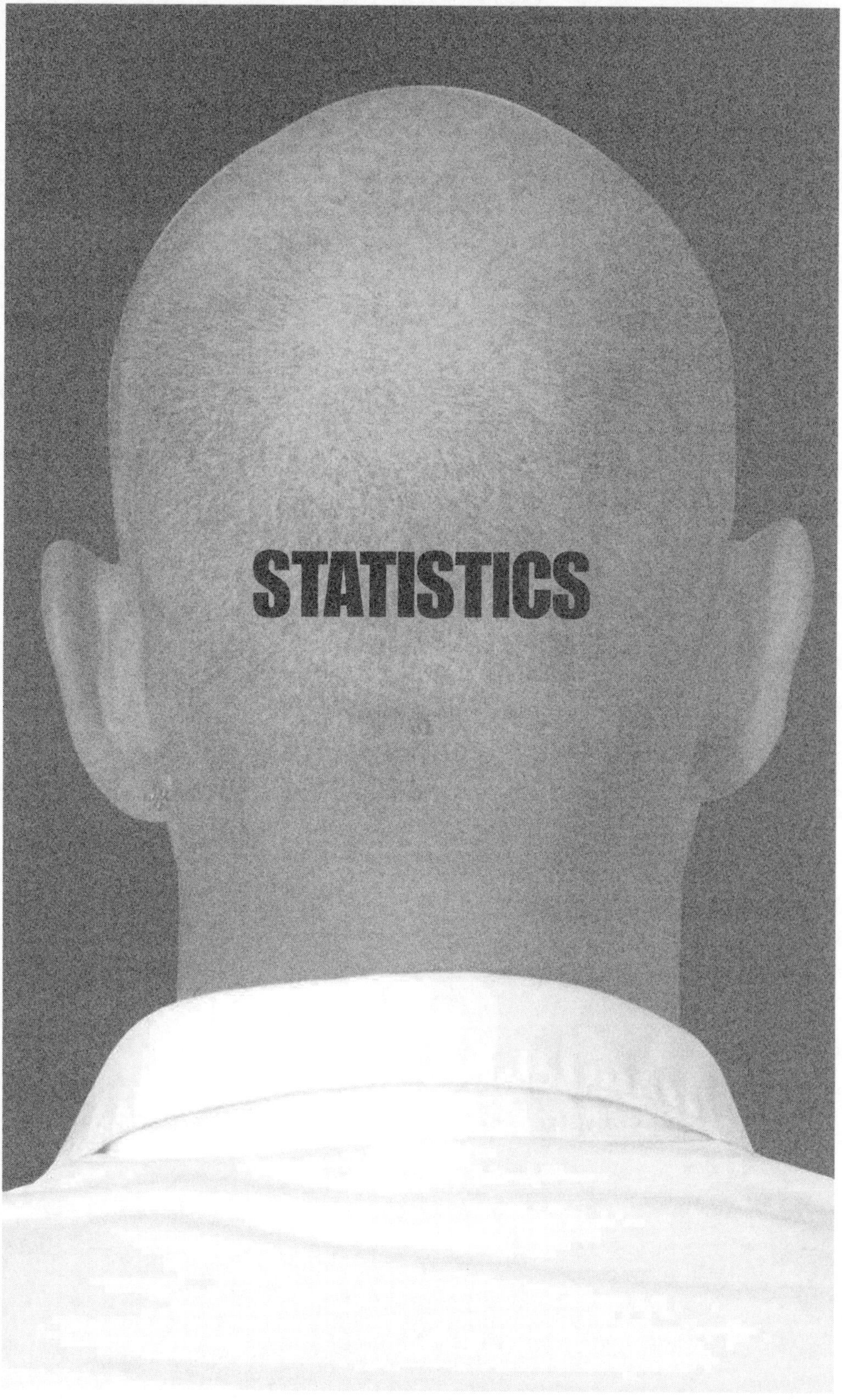
STATISTICS

(Figures accurate to 7 September, 2004)

Darren Scott LEHMANN

(Born: 5 February, 1970, Gawler, South Australia)

Competition	M	Runs	HS	100s	Avge	Ct	Wkt	Avge	BB
Sheffield Shield/									
Pura Cup	125	11,467	255	38	53.84	78	24	48.25	3/42
Test Cricket	20	1,549	177	5	51.63	9	13	22.08	3/42
Other First-Class	94	8,557	252	26	63.39	38	57	31.04	4/35
First-Class	239	21,573	255	69	57.07	125	94	34.19	4/35
One-day Internationals	105	2,848	119	4	39.01	22	44	25.91	4/7
Domestic One-dayers	75	3,095	142*	6	48.36	24	18	30.33	3/16

* Denotes not out; + denotes retired hurt.

BATTING AND FIELDING

FIRST-CLASS
Debut: 1987–88 South Australia v Victoria in Melbourne

Season	Venue	M	Inns	NO	Runs	HS	0s	50s	100s	Avge	Ct
1987-88	Australia	1	1	0	10	10	0	0	0	10.00	0
1988-89	Australia	7	13	1	478	89	1	5	0	39.83	4
1989-90	Australia	12	20	0	1,142	228	1	3	5	57.10	3
1990-91	Australia	10	17	0	626	139	1	3	2	36.82	9
1991	England	1	2	0	23	15	0	0	0	11.50	0
1991-92	Australia	11	19	4	846	148	0	3	3	56.40	9
1992-93	Australia	11	20	1	704	112	0	5	1	37.05	6
1993-94	Australia	11	19	0	1,087	200	0	4	4	57.21	6
1994-95	Australia	11	20	1	1,104	202*	2	6	3	58.11	7
1995-96	Australia	12	23	1	1,237	161	4	6	5	56.23	7
1996-97	Australia	11	19	1	960	255	1	3	2	53.33	7
1997	England	17	27	2	1,575	182	0	10	4	63.00	9
1997-98	Australia	5	8	0	395	138	0	2	1	49.38	5
1997-98	India	3	4	0	132	76	0	2	0	33.00	2
1998	England	10	16	0	969	200	0	4	3	60.56	4
1998-99	Pakistan	3	5	1	330	103	0	1	2	82.50	1
1998-99	Australia	7	12	3	592	175	1	2	2	65.78	4
1999-00	Australia	10	20	2	1,142	149	1	1	7	63.44	3
2000	England	16	23	1	1,477	136	0	9	4	67.14	8
2000-01	Australia	8	16	2	645	146	1	3	1	46.07	4
2001	England	13	19	2	1,416	252	1	5	5	83.29	6

Season	Venue	M	Inns	NO	Runs	HS	0s	50s	100s	Avge	Ct
2001-02	Australia	8	14	0	823	246	2	1	4	58.79	3
2001-02	South Africa	1	1	0	60	60	0	1	0	60.00	0
2002	England	10	18	1	1,136	216	0	7	3	66.82	5
2002-03	Australia	5	8	1	256	97	0	1	0	36.57	3
2002-03	West Indies	5	9	2	439	160	0	2	1	62.71	2
2003-04	Australia	7	11	1	689	237	0	0	3	68.90	5
2003-04	Sri Lanka	4	7	0	509	153	0	1	3	72.71	0
2004	England	7	11	1	592	120	0	5	1	59.20	2
2004-05	Australia	2	4	0	179	57	0	3	0	44.75	1
Total		239	406	28	21,573	255	16	98	69	57.07	125

Country	M	Inns	NO	Runs	HS	0s	50s	100s	Avge	Ct
Australia	149	264	18	12,915	255	15	51	43	52.50	86
England	74	116	7	7,188	252	1	40	20	65.94	34
India	3	4	0	132	76	0	2	0	33.00	2
Pakistan	3	5	1	330	103	0	1	2	82.50	1
South Africa	1	1	0	60	60	0	1	0	60.00	0
Sri Lanka	4	7	0	509	153	0	1	3	72.71	0
West Indies	5	9	2	439	160	0	2	1	62.71	2

Batting Position	Inns	NO	Runs	HS	0s	50s	100s	Avge
1 or 2	5	0	201	67	0	3	0	40.20
3	33	5	1,627	252	2	4	7	58.11
4	254	14	14,532	255	10	64	48	60.55
5	84	2	3,968	202*	3	22	11	48.39
6	26	4	985	228	1	4	2	44.77
7	4	3	260	115	0	1	1	260.00

Team	M	Inns	NO	Runs	HS	0s	50s	100s	Avge	Ct
Australia A	1	1	0	66	66	0	1	0	66.00	0
AUSTRALIA	20	32	2	1,549	177	1	8	5	51.63	9
Australian XI	10	15	43	668	134	0	3	3	60.73	1
South Australia	104	190	11	10,027	255	13	36	35	56.02	57
Victoria	31	54	4	2,098	148	1	10	6	41.96	24
Yorkshire	73	111	7	7,165	252	1	40	20	66.96	34

CENTURIES
Highest Score: 255 South Australia v Queensland in Adelaide, 1996-97

Score	Team	Opponent	Venue	Season
228	South Australia	New South Wales	Adelaide	1989-90
109	South Australia	Sri Lankans	Adelaide	1989-90
128	South Australia	Victoria	Melbourne	1989-90
125	South Australia	Victoria	Adelaide	1989-90

STATISTICS

Score	Team	Opponent	Venue	Season
100	South Australia	Queensland	Adelaide	1989-90
139	Victoria	South Australia	Adelaide	1990-91
113	Victoria	Western Australia	Perth	1990-91
148	Victoria	Western Australia	Melbourne	1991-92
112	Victoria	South Australia	Adelaide	1991-92
137*	Victoria	Queensland	Melbourne	1991-92
112	Victoria	South Australia	Melbourne	1992-93
128	South Australia	Queensland	Brisbane	1993-94
200	South Australia	Western Australia	Adelaide	1993-94
137	South Australia	Tasmania	Hobart	1993-94
157	South Australia	Tasmania	Adelaide	1993-94
109	South Australia	New South Wales	Adelaide	1994-95
100	South Australia	Victoria	Adelaide	1994-95
202*	South Australia	Victoria	Melbourne	1994-95
138	South Australia	Pakistanis	Adelaide	1995-96
116	South Australia	Western Australia	Adelaide	1995-96
103	South Australia	Victoria	Adelaide	1995-96
161	South Australia	Western Australia	Perth	1995-96
105	South Australia	Tasmania	Hobart	1995-96
255	South Australia	Queensland	Adelaide	1996-97
167	South Australia	Victoria	Adelaide	1996-97
177	Yorkshire	Somerset	Taunton	1997
100	Yorkshire	Surrey	The Oval	1997
163*	Yorkshire	Leicestershire	Leicester	1997
182	Yorkshire	Hampshire	Portsmouth	1997
138	South Australia	Tasmania	Adelaide	1997-98
136	Yorkshire	Kent	Maidstone	1998
131	Yorkshire	Nottinghamshire	Scarborough	1998
200	Yorkshire	Worcestershire	Worcester	1998
103	Australian XI	Rawalpindi	Rawalpindi	1998-99
100+	Australian XI	Rawalpindi	Rawalpindi	1998-99
171	South Australia	Victoria	Melbourne	1998-99
175	South Australia	Queensland	Adelaide	1998-99
121	South Australia	New South Wales	Sydney	1999-00
136*	South Australia	Pakistanis	Adelaide	1999-00
120	South Australia	Western Australia	Adelaide	1999-00
101*	South Australia	Tasmania	Hobart	1999-00
113	South Australia	Tasmania	Hobart	1999-00
149	South Australia	Tasmania	Adelaide	1999-00
104	South Australia	Queensland	Albion	1999-00
133	Yorkshire	Derbyshire	Derby	2000
136	Yorkshire	Durham	Leeds	2000
115	Yorkshire	Leicestershire	Leicester	2000
116	Yorkshire	Kent	Canterbury	2000
146	South Australia	New South Wales	Adelaide	2000-01
187*	Yorkshire	Somerset	Bath	2001
104	Yorkshire	Leicestershire	Leeds	2001
252	Yorkshire	Lancashire	Leeds	2001
106*	Yorkshire	Surrey	Leeds	2001
193	Yorkshire	Leicestershire	Leicester	2001
103	South Australia	Victoria	Adelaide	2001-02

DARREN LEHMANN

Score	Team	Opponent	Venue	Season
246	South Australia	Tasmania	Hobart	2001-02
143	South Australia	New South Wales	Adelaide	2001-02
129	South Australia	Queensland	Brisbane	2001-02
119*	Yorkshire	Leicestershire	Leicester	2002
216	Yorkshire	Sussex	Arundel	2002
187	Yorkshire	Lancashire	Leeds	2002
160	AUSTRALIA	WEST INDIES	Port-of-Spain	2002-03
110	AUSTRALIA	BANGLADESH	Darwin	2003-04
177	AUSTRALIA	BANGLADESH	Cairns	2003-04
237	South Australia	New South Wales	Sydney	2003-04
134	Australian XI	Sri Lankan President's XI	Colombo	2003-04
129	AUSTRALIA	SRI LANKA	Galle	2003-04
153	AUSTRALIA	SRI LANKA	Colombo	2003-04
120	Yorkshire	Durham	Chester-le-Street	2004

ONE-DAY INTERNATIONALS
Debut: 1996-97 Australia v Sri Lanka in Colombo

M	Inns	NO	Runs	0s	50s	100s	Avge	S-R	Ct
105	92	19	2,848	3	15	4	39.01	81.49	22

Centuries

Score	Team	Opponent	Venue	Season
103	Australia	Pakistan	Karachi	1998-99
110*	Australia	West Indies	St George's	1998-99
119	Australia	Sri Lanka	Perth	2002-03
107	Australia	West Indies	St George's	2002-03

DOMESTIC ONE-DAYERS
Debut: 1988-89 South Australia v Queensland, Adelaide

M	Inns	NO	Runs	0s	50s	100s	Avge	S-R	Ct
75	74	10	3,095	6	22	6	48.36	86.45	24

Centuries

Score	Team	Opponent	Venue	Season
106*	South Australia	New South Wales	North Sydney	1994-95
142*	South Australia	Tasmania	Adelaide	1994-95
102	South Australia	Western Australia	Adelaide	1994-95
115*	South Australia	New South Wales	North Sydney	2000-01
119*	South Australia	Victoria	Adelaide	2000-01
101	South Australia	New South Wales	Coffs Harbour	2001-02

STATISTICS

BOWLING

Competition	M	Overs	Mdns	Runs	Wkts	Avrge	Best	RPO
Sheffield Shield/Pura Cup	125	392.4	77	1,158	24	48.25	3/42	2.94
Test Cricket	20	123.2	29	287	13	22.08	3/42	2.32
Other First-class	94	634.1	133	1,769	57	31.04	4/35	2.78
First-Class	239	1,150.1	239	3,214	94	34.19	4/35	2.79
One-Day Internationals	105	242.2	2	1,140	44	25.91	4/7	4.70
Domestic One-Dayers	75	105.0	2	546	18	30.33	3/16	5.20

Best Bowling

Sheffield Shield/Pura Cup	3/42 South Australia v Queensland, 2001-02
Test Cricket	3/42 Australia v Zimbabwe, Perth, 2003-04
Other First-class	4/35 Yorkshire v Essex, Chelmsford, 2004
One-Day Internationals	4/7 Australia v Zimbabwe, Perth, 2003-04
Domestic One-Dayers	3/16 South Australia v Victoria, Adelaide, 2001-02

RECORDS

MOST FIRST-CLASS RUNS BY AUSTRALIANS

Batsman	Career	M	Inns	NO	Runs	HS	50s	100s	Avge
D.G. Bradman	1927-28–1948-49	234	338	43	28,067	452*	69	117	95.14
A.R. Border	1976-77–1995-96	385	625	97	27,131	205	142	70	51.38
M.E. Waugh	1985-86–2003-04	368	591	75	26,855	229*	133	81	52.04
G.S. Chappell	1966-67–1983-84	322	542	72	24,535	247*	111	74	52.20
S.R. Waugh	1984-85–2003-04	356	551	88	24,051	216*	97	79	51.95
D.C. Boon	1978-79–1999	350	585	53	23,413	227	114	68	44.01
S.G. Law	1988-89–2004	305	504	56	22,929	263	107	67	51.18
K.J. Grieves	1945-46–1964	490	746	79	22,454	224	136	29	33.66
R.N. Harvey	1946-47–1962-63	306	461	35	21,699	231*	94	67	50.93
D.S. Lehmann	1987-88–2004-05	239	406	28	21,573	255	98	69	57.07
R.B. Simpson	1952-53–1977-78	257	436	62	21,029	359	100	60	56.22
T.M. Moody	1985-86–2000-01	300	501	47	21,001	272	94	64	46.26
J.L. Langer	1991-92–2004-05	253	442	42	20,235	274*	76	64	50.59
M.L. Hayden	1991-92–2004-05	236	408	41	20,180	380	80	68	54.99

MOST FIRST-CLASS CENTURIES BY AUSTRALIANS

Batsman	Career	M	Inns	100s	Inns per 100
D.G. Bradman	1927-28–1948-49	234	338	117	2.89
M.E. Waugh	1985-86–2003-04	368	591	81	7.29
G.S. Chappell	1966-67–1983-84	322	542	74	7.32
S.R. Waugh	1984-85–2003-04	356	551	79	6.97
A.R. Border	1976-77–1995-96	385	625	70	8.92
D.S. Lehmann	1987-88–2004-05	239	406	69	5.88
D.C. Boon	1978-79–1999	350	585	68	8.60
M.L. Hayden	1991-92–2004-05	236	408	68	6.00
R.N. Harvey	1946-47–1962-63	306	461	67	6.88
S.G. Law	1988-89–2004	305	504	67	7.52
T.M. Moody	1985-86–2000-01	300	501	64	7.82
J.L. Langer	1991-92–2004-05	253	442	64	6.90
R.B. Simpson	1952-53–1977-78	257	436	60	7.27

MOST FIRST-CLASS RUNS FOR ONE STATE

Batsman	State	M	Inns	NO	Runs	HS	50s	100s	Avge
J. Cox	Tas	163	294	18	11,450	245	47	34	41.49
D.W. Hookes	SA	136	233	10	10,439	306*	50	29	46.81
D.M. Jones	Vic	124	217	17	10,412	324*	42	33	52.06
D.S. Lehmann	SA	104	190	11	10,027	255	36	35	56.02
S.G. Law	Qld	158	261	31	9,920	216	53	25	43.13
L.E. Favell	SA	143	258	5	9,656	164	51	23	38.16
T.M. Moody	WA	145	247	22	9,520	272	49	21	42.31
S.C. Trimble	Qld	133	246	14	9,465	252*	44	24	40.79
G.S. Blewett	SA	107	203	11	9,379	268	44	26	48.85
M.G. Bevan	NSW	105	183	36	9,309	216	35	37	63.33
M.T.G. Elliott	Vic	97	185	16	9,099	203	39	31	53.84
D.C. Boon	Tas	139	235	14	9,096	227	46	22	41.16

MOST FIRST-CLASS APPEARANCES FOR SOUTH AUSTRALIA

Player	Career	Matches
P.R. Sleep	1976-77–1992-93	146
L.E. Favell	1951-52–1969-70	143
D.W. Hookes	1975-76–1991-92	136
H.N. Dansie	1949-50–1966-67	124
I.M. Chappell	1961-62–1979-80	109
G.S. Blewett	1991-92–2003-04	107
C.V. Grimmett	1924-25–1940-41	105
V.Y. Richardson	1918-19–1937-38	104
D.S. Lehmann	1987-88–2003-04	104
A.M.J. Hilditch	1982-83–1991-92	102

MOST FIRST-CLASS RUNS FOR SOUTH AUSTRALIA

Batsman	M	Inns	NO	Runs	HS	50s	100s	Avge
D.W. Hookes	136	233	10	10,439	306*	50	29	46.81
D.S. Lehmann	104	190	11	10,027	255	36	35	56.02
L.E. Favell	143	258	5	9,656	164	51	23	38.16
G.S. Blewett	107	203	11	9,379	268	44	26	48.85
I.M. Chappell	109	188	18	8,873	205*	51	26	52.19
C. Hill	87	160	9	8,027	365*	37	24	53.15
V.Y. Richardson	104	188	7	7,698	231	38	21	42.53
H.N. Dansie	124	228	9	7,543	185	36	18	34.44
P.R. Sleep	146	244	45	6,982	146*	34	13	35.08
A.M.J. Hilditch	102	182	12	6,938	230	34	17	40.81

MOST SHEFFIELD SHIELD/PURA CUP APPEARANCES

Player	State	Career	Matches
R.J. Inverarity	WA/SA	1962-63–1984-85	159
J. Cox	Tas	1987-88–2003-04	153
J.D. Siddons	Vic/SA	1984-85–1999-00	146
S.G. Law	Qld	1988-89–2003-04	142

STATISTICS

Player	State	Career	Matches
D.S. Berry	SA/Vic	1989-90–2003-04	139
T.M. Moody	WA	1985-86–2000-01	132
P.R. Sleep	SA	1976-77–1992-93	127
D.S. Lehmann	SA/Vic	1987-88–2003-04	125
S.C. Trimble	Qld	1959-60–1975-76	123
L.E. Favell	SA	1951-52–1969-70	120
D.W. Hookes	SA	1975-76–1991-92	120

MOST SHEFFIELD SHIELD/PURA CUP RUNS

Batsman	State	M	Inns	NO	Runs	HS	50s	100s	Avge
D.S. Lehmann	SA/Vic	125	227	14	11,467	255	44	38	53.84
J.D. Siddons	Vic/SA	146	259	21	10,643	245	50	30	44
J. Cox	Tas	153	279	17	10,459	245	44	30	39.92
D.M. Jones	Vic	110	194	16	9,622	324*	40	31	54.06
D.W. Hookes	SA	120	205	9	9,364	306*	44	26	47.78
R.J. Inverarity	WA/SA	159	275	32	9,341	187	45	22	38.44
S.G. Law	Qld	142	234	28	9,034	216	47	24	43.85
D.G. Bradman	NSW/SA	62	96	15	8,926	452*	20	36	110.19
M.T.G. Elliott	Vic	93	178	16	8,885	203	38	31	54.85
T.M. Moody	WA	132	228	22	8,853	272	46	20	42.98

MOST SHEFFIELD SHIELD/PURA CUP APPEARANCES FOR SOUTH AUSTRALIA

Player	Career	Matches
P.R. Sleep	1976-77–1992-93	127
L.E. Favell	1951-52–1969-70	121
D.W. Hookes	1975-76–1991-92	120
H.N. Dansie	1949-50–1966-67	107
G.S. Blewett	1991-92–2003-04	100
D.S. Lehmann	1987-88–2003-04	97
T.J. Nielsen	1990-91–1998-99	92
A.M.J. Hilditch	1982-83–1991-92	91
I.M. Chappell	1961-62–1979-80	89
G.A. Bishop	1982-83–1992-93	84

MOST SHEFFIELD SHIELD/PURA CUP RUNS FOR SOUTH AUSTRALIA

Batsman	M	Inns	NO	Runs	HS	50s	100s	Avge
D.S. Lehmann	97	179	10	9,454	255	34	32	55.94
D.W. Hookes	120	205	9	9,364	306*	44	26	47.78
G.S. Blewett	100	190	10	8,794	268	43	23	48.86
L.E. Favell	121	220	4	8,269	164	43	20	38.28
I.M. Chappell	89	157	13	7,665	205*	45	22	53.23
H.N. Dansie	107	196	6	6,692	185	32	17	35.22
A.M.J. Hilditch	91	161	11	6,504	230	32	17	43.36
C. Hill	68	126	6	6,270	365*	27	18	52.25
P.R. Sleep	127	211	37	6,106	146*	29	12	35.09
V.Y. Richardson	77	146	7	6,027	203	27	18	43.36

MOST DOMESTIC ONE-DAY APPEARANCES

Player	State	Career	Matches
D.S. Berry	SA/Vic	1989-90–2003-04	87
S.G. Law	Qld	1988-89–2003-04	85
G.S. Blewett	SA	1992-93–2003-04	79
J.L. Langer	WA	1992-93–2003-04	78
M.L. Love	Qld	1993-94–2003-04	78
J. Cox	Tas	1988-89–2003-04	75
M.J. Di Venuto	Tas	1997-98–2003-04	75
B.J. Hodge	Vic	1993-94–2003-04	75
D.S. Lehmann	SA/Vic	1988-89–2003-04	75
T.M. Moody	WA	1985-86–2000-01	75

MOST DOMESTIC ONE-DAY RUNS

Batsman	State	M	Inns	NO	Runs	HS	50s	100s	Avge	S-R
J.P. Maher	Qld	73	73	9	3,137	187	17	7	49.02	77.73
D.S. Lehmann	SA/Vic	75	74	10	3,095	142*	22	6	48.36	86.45
J.L. Langer	WA	78	74	6	2,815	146	19	6	41.40	69.08
G.S. Blewett	SA	79	77	7	2,740	109*	17	3	39.14	66.78
B.J. Hodge	Vic	75	73	8	2,643	118*	16	6	40.66	73.62
S.G. Law	Qld	85	78	7	2,534	159	10	6	35.69	93.06
M.G. Bevan	SA/NSW	60	60	20	2,478	135*	22	1	61.95	73.05
M.L. Love	Qld	78	75	10	2,315	127*	9	4	35.62	76.99
M.T.G. Elliott	Vic	68	66	6	2,247	118*	12	6	37.45	70.44
S.R. Waugh	NSW	55	54	10	2,269	131	13	5	51.57	84.26

ACKNOWLEDGEMENTS

I wish to thank those people who made this book possible. Without their help and guidance, I could never have achieved it.

Firstly, to James Brayshaw for his endless and tiring work: this whole thing would have been impossible without your immense help and input. For countless enjoyable hours of reminiscing – many thanks mate.

Mary Small of Hardie Grant Books, thank you for being so supportive and patient with me, and for all your help through the whole process. Bloody computers – maybe next time I will get one that works properly from anywhere in the world! Mary, you have been a champ.

To everyone at Hardie Grant Books, many thanks. Sandy, thanks for taking this on and talking me through it all.

Andrea, my beautiful wife, thank you for helping me through the times when I thought this book was getting too tough to write, and for the many hours helping me with the bloody computers. I love you very much.

Ricky Ponting and Adam Gilchrist, thank you for your generous words in the forewords. You have been fantastic colleagues to play with, and magnificent friends.

There are many people who may not have helped me write this book, but who I am forever grateful to for making me happy doing a job I love. To my team-mates – past and present – of the Australian, South Australian, Victorian, Yorkshire and Northern Districts cricket teams, thank you for all the memories and laughs along the way. I am honoured to have been given the opportunity to play alongside each of you.

To Macca, Struds and Blewy: thanks for your true and unwavering friendship. Mahbo and Harvs – could we laugh any more? Thanks guys, for the good times and also the support in the bad times.

To Greg Chappell, Wayne Clark, Wayne Phillips, John Buchanan and Tim Neilsen: a bloke couldn't ask for better coaches. Thanks for always pushing me to greater heights, but also for all your friendship and support.

To all at the SACA, and I mean all departments, not just cricket: you've been there throughout my entire career. Thanks for all the support, and for taking great care of me. Thanks also to all South Australian cricket fans who have supported me through the good, but importantly through the bad and uncertain times. I am immensely grateful, and very proud to play cricket for South Australia.

To Cricket Australia: thanks for the opportunity to play for my country and allowing me my dream, and also to all who have supported me and my family with the many arrangements over the years.

To my great friends at Yorkshire County Cricket Club who have been fantastic throughout the years I've played there. Thanks to all for looking after us in our home away from home. To the boys: you blokes really know how to make a guy feel welcome, and how to make him laugh!

To Chalks: bro, thanks, and looking forward to many more good times together. Much appreciation to you and Liz for all your support for our family, and for the many brilliant times we've had together.

To T. D.: mate, many thanks for all your help and friendship over the years.

ACKNOWLEDGEMENTS

To all my sponsors over my many years of playing, I thank you all for your support. I particularly wish to thank my long-term sponsors Greg Smythe from Gray Nicholls and George Lawlor from Nike, for always going the extra mile and making life on the road so much easier.

On the home front, to my family and friends who have all supported me in so many ways I can never express enough gratitude. Many of you also help out Andrea and the kids while I am so often away, and for this I am eternally grateful. Dad, for all your love and positive thinking, I love you. To my stepfather, Dennis: thank you for always going the extra yards to help me and Andrea, and for taking such great care of my mum. To my grandparents for all your support in my early days, and also for helping out and being there in recent times.

To cricket fans worldwide: thanks for supporting me throughout my career and for coming to the games. Hopefully we, as cricketers, entertain you well because without your prescence in the stands this game wouldn't be half as fun.